P9-DTY-278

At Prayer
with
Mother
Teresa

At Prayer
with
Mother Teresa

E I L E E N   E G A N

Liguori
LIGUORI, MISSOURI

Published by Liguori Publications
Liguori, Missouri
http://www.liguori.org

Compiled and Edited by Judy Bauer

Grateful acknowledgment is hereby made to *America* magazine for permission to print in revised form material that had previously appeared in that publication.

Library of Congress Cataloging-in-Publication Data

Egan, Eileen.

   At prayer with Mother Teresa / Eileen Egan : compiled and edited by Judy Bauer.
      p. cm.
   ISBN 0-7648-0339-5
   1. Prayers. 2. Teresa, Mother, 1910– . I. Bauer, Judy, 1941– . II. Title
BV245.E43   1999
242'.802—dc21   98–37434

Printed in the United States of America
03 02 01 00 99   5 4 3 2

Prayer for Prayer

Mother Teresa wrote much on prayer. For example, she instructed her sisters to improve their spirit of prayer and recollection during Lent. She told them: "Let us free our minds from all that is not Jesus. If you find it difficult to pray, ask Him again and again."

> *Jesus come into my heart,*
> *Pray with me,*
> *Pray in me—*
> *That I my learn from Thee*
> *How to pray.*

Contents

Part I

Introduction

The small, worn body of Mother Teresa wrapped in the blue-bordered white sari was poised atop a gun carriage as it wound its way through the streets of Calcutta. The same gun carriage had carried the body of the murdered Gandhi, whom Mother Teresa, in common with the people of her adopted country, called "The Father of Our Country."

At the beginning of 1948, the world had mourned the loss of the Indian man of peace. At the end of 1948, an unknown woman had stepped out alone on Calcutta's scourged streets moved by a call to merge her life with "the poorest of the poor."

Now the government of India had decreed a state funeral for Mother Teresa. Televised throughout the world was the cortege as it moved along the streets of shops and businesses, and the roads that skirted Calcutta's lung, the great park known as the Maidan. While it missed the slum areas, the poor came to join those who thronged the streets to honor the woman who had symbolized merciful, loving help and asked nothing in return.

In India, the very sight of a holy person is considered to confer a sort of blessing. This is called "darshan." Could the sight of this small figure confer a sort of "darshan" on the peoples of the world who would see her for the last time?

After a funeral mass that filled the stadium, a mass attended by dignitaries of many countries, including the wife of the American president, Mrs. Hillary Rodham Clinton, the cortege drove up to the Motherhouse of the Missionaries of Charity. The gate was opened to receive a small number of those who took part in the funeral and the coffin of Mother Teresa. Then the gate was shut. In the courtyard of the Motherhouse a grave had been prepared.

It was at that gate that Mother Teresa had appeared in answer to my ringing of a bell in 1955. We sat in rickety chairs in the little parlor as she told me of the work of the Missionaries of Charity. After visiting a home for sick and homeless children, a leprosy center, a slum school, and a health clinic for the poorest of mothers, Mother Teresa said, "Now I want to take you to my treasures."

Through the noise-filled, jampacked streets of Calcutta we made our way to the pilgrims' hostel of the Temple of Kali. Pilgrims to the shrine of the black-visaged goddess of destruction, with her necklace of skulls, came and went through a door nearby, while we visited with pilgrims who were approaching another door, the door of death.

In one section of the hostel, about forty men lay side by

side on pallets lining both sides of a dropped walkway. In the other section was a similar number of women. The hostel itself was the type of caravanserai used by poor travelers on ancient trade routes and had been intended for the poorest pilgrims who had journeyed to make their *puja* (act of homage) to Kali.

Mother Teresa had brought me to the Home for the Dying. As we went along the walkway, she stopped at a pallet and, seating herself on the raised parapet, caressed the head of a cadaverous man from whom all had been taken but breath itself. His skull seemed ready to burst through the skin and his great black eyes were locked in a fixed stare. When she took in her hands the paper-thin hands of men or women she communicated with them by the consoling stroke of her strong fingers. Some sat up, looking around as though surprised to be alive.

Meanwhile, a band of young Indian women, also in white saris, were busy among the patients, washing them or lifting their heads to feed them, spoonful by spoonful. These charges were the men and women picked up from the streets of a scourged city—host to a million refugees displaced a few years earlier at the partition of the Indian subcontinent. They beggared the resources of the Calcutta community. "We could not let them die like animals in the street," said Mother Teresa. "The Corporation of Calcutta gave us this hostel. Here they die loved and cared for."

As I followed Mother Teresa, a few waving hands were held out to me, expecting that I, too, would stop for a consoling touch. I knew that along with starvation most of the diseases known to humankind were in that enclosure. I was shortly to leave for Vietnam. Trembling and ashamed, I turned away.

I also knew that from 1952 onward Mother Teresa and her sisters had been cleaning the rotting sores and removing the maggots and spittle from men and women found dying on the streets. Often unable to give anything more than a humane death, they treated these patients in their last hours as children of God.

I wondered aloud how they could do this day after day. "Our work," Mother Teresa explained, "calls for us to see Jesus in everyone. Jesus has told us that he is the hungry one, the naked one, the thirsty one. He is the one without a home. He is the one who is suffering."

She looked around at the rows of pallets in the caravanserai. "They are Jesus. Each one is Jesus in a distressing disguise." She said it with a sort of luminous conviction. As I came to know more of her work and saw it grow in India and the world, I realized that this conviction was its bedrock. Each person was to be treated as a repository of the divine. If disfigured by the filth of the street, by leprosy, by anything that diminished his or her dignity, the person had to be envisioned in the light of the divinity behind the disguise. The infinite inviolable dignity was always the same.

BEGINNINGS

Mother Teresa's work and her foundation in 1959 of a new congregation called the Missionaries of Charity arose from an inspiration that came to her on a train taking her in September 1946 from Calcutta to Darjeeling in the Himalayas. For almost twenty years she had been a member of the Institute of the Blessed Virgin Mary, commonly known as the Sisters of Loreto, and many of those years had been spent in classrooms of the various schools of the congregation. She was on her way to make her annual retreat.

The Motherhouse of Loreto in Dublin had been her introduction to the Institute she joined at eighteen years of age, a young woman of Albanian origin born in 1910 in the town of Skopje in what became, after World War I, Yugoslavia. Her devout mother, whose works of mercy went so far as to bring suffering people into her own home, was a decisive influence in her life. After leaving home, Agnes Gonxha Bojaxhiu (as she had been baptized) was never to see her mother again. Skopje, a city where East and West met, with its many mosques, a number of richly decorated Orthodox churches and a few churches for the Catholic minority, had served, in a way, as a preparation for Calcutta.

During the years between 1929, when she arrived in Calcutta, and 1947, the time of her retreat, Mother Teresa had known the agony that had descended on a great city. In 1943, the war-borne Bengal famine brought death to several million people. In August 1946, on the Day of the Great Killing, Muslims and Hindus inflamed by political rhetoric turned on each other. Bloodshed brought the city to a standstill. Despite a curfew, Mother Teresa braved the streets to obtain food for her boarding school students. What she saw appalled her.

On the train to Darjeeling, Mother Teresa received what she referred to as "a call within a call"—to leave the enclosed life of a sister—teacher in order to work on the streets. The constitution of the Missionaries of Charity states: "Our religious family started when our foundress, Mother M. Teresa Bojaxhiu, was inspirited by the Holy Spirit on the tenth of September, 1946. This inspiration, or charism, means that the Holy Spirit communicated God's will to Mother."

Coming down from Darjeeling that September, the Sister of Loreto who had been the principal of St. Mary's High School in Calcutta, explained to her congregation, to the Archbishop of Calcutta, and to her Jesuit Advisor, Celeste Van Exem, that her future was to be on the streets of Calcutta. But before her "call within a call" could begin to find expression, a two-year process was necessary. She wrote to Rome for permission to leave the Loreto congregation. She requested "exclaustration," which meant that she would continue to live as a vowed nun. The Archbishop of Calcutta, however, insisted on changing the word to "secularization," meaning she would no longer be a sister under vows but a laywoman. This would have placed an almost insurmountable obstacle to the later founding of a congregation. The future Missionaries of Charity hung by a thread. Unaccountably, when the permission arrived, it said "exclaustration."

Many years later, the mystery was solved. In 1971, Mother Teresa and I talked with the Apostolic Delegate in Washington, D.C., Archbishop Luigi Raimondi. He had been serving as counselor in Delhi when Mother Teresa's letter arrived. Accompanying the letter, he told us, was a letter from the Archbishop of Calcutta. The diplomat explained that, noting the favorable content of the Archbishop's letter and the fact that the request was for a year's trial, he decided to grant the permission from Delhi rather than forward the request to Rome. He made no mention of the change in wording, nor did Mother Teresa raise the question. If this request had been routinely referred to Rome, the reply would surely have been handled in a routine manner, and "secularization" would have stood.

On August 16, 1948, exactly two years after the Day of the Great Killing, Mother Teresa went to Patna for a short course in nursing with the Medical Missionary Sisters, a group founded in the United States by Mother Anna Dengel, M.D., in 1925. The voluminous habit of the Sisters of Loreto was replaced by the rough cotton sari of the poor. On her left shoulder a small crucifix was affixed with a safety pin. On her stockingless feet were sandals. The Little Sisters of the Poor gave her shelter. On December 21, 1948, she stepped out alone into the abyss of her new life, making her way to the fetid slum that abutted the compound of the boarding school where she had once taught. She was thirty-eight years of age.

Around her, in the Moti Jihl slum, she gathered the illiterate, nearly naked children, and, sitting on a chair, drilled them in the letters of the Bengali alphabet while marking the outlines in the dust with a stick.

In 1927 Mohandas Gandhi has suggested a way of life to Christians in India. "Let them start at the bottom....In a word, let them go to the people not as patrons, but as one of them, not to oblige them, but to serve them and to work among them." Mother Teresa did indeed "start at the bottom," but she went further with a step revolutionary for a woman who was a European missionary. She became one with the people by asking for and receiving Indian citizenship in 1948.

GROWTH

It was not until March 1949 that two of her former students joined her. A Bengali Catholic family gave them a home, and soon a group of twelve young women joined Mother Teresa in opening slum schools. When the monsoons came, they had to find shelter. Father Van Exem collected funds for the rent of schoolrooms in the slums. From the beginning, the language of the sisters was English.

On their way to the school, Mother Teresa and the sisters had to pass whole families living on the street. Often a lone man or woman would be fighting for a last breath in the gutter. That was when they rented rooms in Moti Jihl and cleaned and fed the hapless people until death released them or until they found enough strength to return to the street.

Then, in October 1950, the Missionaries of Charity were recognized as a religious society, limited to the Archdiocese of Calcutta.

When I was asked to write an account of the work of the Missionaries of Charity for Mother Teresa's Co-Workers, she dictated the following: "In the choice of works, there was neither planning nor preconceived ideas. We started the work as the suffering of the people called us. God showed us what to do."

Mother Teresa's response to the call of the suffering people in Calcutta set a pattern for the work she would carry out in other cities of India and later in centers of need around the world. On successive visits to Calcutta as a representative of the overseas arm of the U.S. Catholic agency, Catholic Relief Services, I was able to observe the growth of the work and the yearly increase of American Catholic aid to India.

One of the first of the food programs begun by Mother Teresa was for helpless squatters in Sealdah Railroad Station, the terminus of the Eastern Railway from East Pakistan (later Bangladesh) where thousands of destitute newcomers lived. They were part of an unending stream of men, women, and children from "the Dhaka side," who came to the great mother city of Bengal, Calcutta, for refuge. As Indian authorities moved them to refugee camps, new squatters settled themselves on the stone floor of the cavernous waiting room, using the Sealdah washroom for drinking water and hygiene. Many families heated rice and bulgur wheat on tiny mud stoves. Tons of these grains were shipped to Calcutta and other ports of India by Catholic Relief Services. "They get used to the bulgur wheat, but they prefer the rice," Mother Teresa told me as we moved through the steaming pit of misery, a prototype of Calcutta's famous "black hole."

Mother Teresa also led her sisters to the clusters of lepers in the most desolate slums. There was no leprosarium in

Calcutta, and the priests of the Kali temple had understandably decided that no lepers were to be housed in the hostel. An ambulance donated by an American priest carried doctors from the Institute for Tropical Medicine along with sister-nurses to these slums, close to the shrine of Hanuman the monkey god. I saw how claw-like hands reached for packages of food after each treatment. After some years, the gift of land in a rural area of Bengal allowed Mother Teresa to found a leper village, Shantinagar (Town of Peace).

As they moved about in the poorest districts of Calcutta, the Missionaries of Charity found infants abandoned in alleyways and garbage cans. A home, Shishu Bhavan (Children's Home), was opened next door to a building that was to become the congregation's motherhouse.

Women doctors offered their services to Mother Teresa for the Children's Home and were soon staffing mother-and-child clinics in various poor districts. (It was an absolute necessity that there be a woman doctor in attendance in the Muslim quarters.)

Within a few years, the Missionaries of Charity, constantly increasing in numbers, with candidates from every caste and part of India, were working in fifty-nine Calcutta centers. They brought consolation, healing, education, and, above all, love where suffering abounded. In all their works they were carrying out the fourth vow of the Missionaries of Charity. In addition to the usual promises of poverty, chastity and obedience, they vowed "to give wholehearted and free service to the poorest of the poor."

Part of the sisters' training consisted in this work, but

along with it went rigorous spiritual training. Father Van Exem has often been referred to as a sort of co-founder of the Missionaries of Charity. He helped draw up the rule, later elaborated into a 120-page constitution. Since the Diocese of Calcutta had been entrusted to the Society of Jesus, other Jesuits helped in the spiritual formation of the young women.

The rule, however, expressed the vision of Mother Teresa herself. It emphasized that the Missionaries of Charity would "remain right on the ground by living Christ's concern for the poorest and lowliest." They would continue their work "only until there may be others who can help them in a better and more lasting way." The rule listed the works of mercy, corporal and spiritual, and stated that the sisters, in carrying them out, proved their love of Jesus "under the appearance of bread and under the distressing disguise of the poorest of the poor."

"Our lives are women about the Eucharist," Mother Teresa explained. Every dawn, the sisters began their day with Communion at the table of the Lord. Each sister had a copy of the rule, and she should cling to it, said Mother Teresa, "as a child clings to its mother."

OVERSEAS EXPANSION

When in 1965 the Missionaries of Charity were recognized as a congregation that could work anywhere in the world, there were three hundred sisters, almost all of them Indian. It was a dramatic moment when Indian citizens presented themselves to the Indian Government requesting passports for overseas missions. For India, long a receiver of Christian missionaries from Western countries, the situation was suddenly reversed.

The first overseas invitation to Mother Teresa had its beginning in a conversation of bishops at the Second Vatican Council. A Venezuelan bishop needed sisters to work in a remote area of his country where Afro-Venezuelans, owners of rich land, were threatened with exploitation. Mother Teresa went on ahead to assay the need and to talk to priests who could celebrate Mass for the sisters and provide guidance. When the six Indian sisters arrived, local people prepared a cozy home for them. Piece by piece, the overstuffed sofa, the comfortable chairs, and the frilled curtains were given away to poor families. The sisters explained that their vow of poverty called for more simplicity. Wherever they went, the sisters thanked donors who welcomed them with what seemed to be necessary comforts, like washing machines in Western countries, and then explained why they could not accept these gifts. This simplified way of life meant that sisters could be sent from a house in New York City to one in Papua, New Guinea, without having developed any reliance on consumer comforts unavailable in the new area. They fulfilled their vow of poverty with a sort of spectacular élan.

There was some surprise when in 1971 the Missionaries of Charity responded to the call of Cardinal Terence Cooke to come to New York. They made their first home in Harlem, with the Handmaids of Mary, a religious congregation of black women. The Missionaries of Charity numbered five, four Indians and one sister of German origin, Sister Andrea, who was also a physician. They came with their mattresses and cooking utensils, like the poorest nineteenth-century immigrants. Their first task was to get to know the neighborhood, visiting families and people who lived alone. The Indian sisters were puzzled when they were taken at first to be women of the Nation of Islam.

That was the year when Malcolm Muggeridge's *Something Beautiful for God* was published. This eloquent, vividly illustrated book brought the work of Mother Teresa to world attention. The Missionaries of Charity were soon receiving invitations from bishops on all continents. When teams of sisters left the Calcutta motherhouse, they carried with them the Calcutta plan of response, putting into practice the clear guidance of their rule. They began their work without delay—visiting and washing the old and handicapped and cleaning their living quarters.

Nobody resented them, since they were not taking away anyone's work. I saw how the sisters were accepted in Cairo, where, out beyond the City of the Dead, they went to the great dumping-ground to serve the community of garbage-pickers. There, amid dirt and the odors of things rotting, whole families subsisted by sifting usable items from mounds of debris around them. The sisters' clinic was a busy place, filled with mothers and children needing care for myriad ailments.

In Bourke, Australia, I visited the sisters who lived near a reserve of the aboriginal people. The training center for aboriginal women was well attended, and the sisters were ready to provide other services, including driving sick people to medical centers and sending a van to pick up children who were far from regular attendants at the local school.

When the documentary film "Mother Teresa," produced by Petrie Films, was shown in Moscow, the door to what was then the Soviet Union was opened for the Missionaries of Charity. Once inside the U.S.S.R., where mercy *(miloserdiye),* both the word and the practice, had been banished by a system that outlawed religious charitable activity, the Missionaries of Charity were welcomed from Leningrad to Armenia, from Tbilisi to Novosirsk, Siberia. Even Albania, as tightly closed to the outside world as a maximum security prison, suddenly shed its ideology and opened its doors.

One of the buildings offered to her in Tirana, the Albanian capital, turned out to be a former mosque. "It was uncared for, very dirty," Mother Teresa told me. "The sisters scrubbed and cleaned it out and made sure that the men got new quarters. Then we turned it back to the Muslims. They began prayer there."

In 1985 Mother Teresa told me: "I never expected that I would open a Kalighat [Home for the Dying] in New York City. When I heard that people were dying of this terrible new disease, I knew we must do something. We care for the dying in Kalighat, and that must be our work in New York, too. I found that the dying are mostly young men, and that some of the dying are in prison." The "terrible new disease" was AIDS.

On Christmas Eve 1985 Mother Teresa helped an emaciated man up the steps to a hospice in Greenwich Village. He was the first man to die in the care of the Missionaries of Charity in New York. The New York hospice was the first of six small hospices for AIDS opened by the sisters in the following years. The others were in Baltimore, Philadelphia, Washington, Denver, and San Francisco. In New York City the sisters worked closely with the AIDS service of St. Vincent's Hospital, and in other cities they had the cooperation of local hospitals. These AIDS hospices are among the twenty-seven small centers conducted by the Missionaries of Charity across the United States.

Observers of the work of Mother Teresa have marveled that the work of her congregation could have been implanted in 477 centers over 103 countries in little more than a quarter of a century. For Mother Teresa, the explanation was to be found in one word—providence. She never dwelt on difficulties, although there were many. "God," she said, "is indeed overwhelmingly good to us. He answers our needs even before we have voiced them....There is a miracle almost every day."

She would recall, for instance, how a patient's need for a particular medicine was answered when that medicine appeared at the top of a box of donated medical supplies. The "miracle of the bread" occurred during one of my stays in Calcutta. An out-of-season monsoon almost brought the city to a halt. For the thousands who regularly brought their containers to be filled from the gruel vats in the courtyard of the Shishu Bhavan there was nothing. The people stood drenched and waiting. Because Calcutta's schools were closed, CARE's school feeding program could not operate. The CARE office decided to donate all the food to Mother Teresa's people. Trucks large enough to move through the flooded streets brought thousands upon thousands of loaves of bread, wrapped and fresh, to the courtyard of Shishu Bhavan, and the long lines of people were fed.

The greater mystery was in another order, the order of the transcendent. It is a great gift to "cleanse the doors of perception," as Mother Teresa was able to do, so that one can see Christ in every human being. To transmit that vision to others so that the result is a complete transformation of life is a mystery beyond telling, a mystery of grace. The rule reminds the sisters that "we who enter the ministries of Christ's life ought to be molded into his image until he is formed in us" (Gal 4:19). In Mother Teresa's words, "Just as the seed is meant to be a tree, so are we meant to be Jesus." Those who grow into Jesus grow into the grace of seeing Jesus behind any and every disguise.

Mother Teresa, besides transmitting the vision to women of every race of humankind who joined her, did the same for the Missionary Brothers, the Missionary Fathers, and the lay Co-Workers of Mother Teresa.

PERSONAL RECOGNITION

Since I spent considerable time with Mother Teresa, I have often been asked what she was really like. Of all of her qualities, the most striking to me was her emptiness. She seemed to have no needs of her own, but to be ready to respond to any need around her, ready to be a channel of healing to those who came to her almost inconsolable in their sorrow. Her recollection in the face of emergencies, including helter-skelter drives through city traffic to an airport, was an unforgettable lesson to those who traveled with her. No matter how great the commotion around her, Mother Teresa seemed to be at rest, her mind and heart centered on Jesus. Knowing that she had faced the ultimate in human misery, people posed to her the perennial problem of a loving God and the suffering of his creatures.

"All that suffering—where would we be without it?" she once asked. "It is an innocent suffering and that is the same as the suffering of Jesus. He suffered for us and all that innocent suffering is joined to his in the redemption. It is co-redemption. This is helping to save the world from worse things." In such a belief, the cross of Jesus is behind every stricken and agonizing human body so that none of the seemingly useless suffering is lost in the divine economy.

Attention to Mother Teresa grew as she received honorary degrees and medals, including the Ceres Medal of the U.N. Food and Agriculture Organization. The Pope John XXIII Peace Prize brought her a large fund, as did the Templeton Prize for Progress in Religion. During her seventieth year, being awarded the 1979 Nobel Peace Prize made her name and work even better known around the world. When she reached her seventieth birthday in August 1980, her face appeared on millions of Indian postage stamps.

All the honors were a matter of indifference to her. "I am not the centerpiece of prize-giving day," Mother Teresa remarked. "It is Christ using me to unite all the people present. I feel that to bring all these people together to talk about God is really wonderful." She was grateful, however, that the Nobel Peace Prize recognized works of mercy as works of peace.

In many places in the United States, including New York City, she was given the key to the city. The ceremony was strange to her. In one presentation, she was told that she was "the first citizen of the city." Afterward, to a few Co-Workers, she remarked: "Yesterday, I was the first citizen, and I said, 'Thank you very much.' But I don't understand what it means. It makes no difference; it is coming from the same hand. And tomorrow, if people should say, 'Crucify'— all right. It is the same loving hand. The acceptance for you and for me. It is what Jesus wants from us. To allow him to use us without consulting us."

Criticism of her and her work did come. In Latin America, attacks focused on her because she was concerned for the individual person rather than combatting the structures causing poverty. She answers simply—pointing to the distinction in ministries, "If people feel it is their vocation to change structures, then that is the work they must do."

CHANGES IN OUTLOOK

Over the years, I noted three ways in which Mother Teresa altered her outlook. One concerned the gathering of funds for her work. When groups of supporters called Co-Workers were formed, they were on fire with the need to collect funds to feed the hungry and provide medicines for the sick. There were plans for benefits to further the work. To their surprise, they received the word from Mother Teresa, "No collecting."

These ecumenical Co-Workers charged no dues. Their family-type association was conducted by volunteers who shared the vision of Mother Teresa. They took part in the work of the Missionaries of Charity if they were in the area. If not, they went out in the spirit of Mother Teresa to lighten the load of men, women, and children who knew the world at its worst. Inevitably, funds were given to the Co-Workers, who channeled them to the sisters. Co-Worker groups kept in touch through cheaply produced newsletters. An international newsletter, carrying stories from some groups in seventy countries, was produced by Dr. Warren Kump and his wife, Patricia, of Minneapolis, Minnesota. The cost of printing and mailing it around the world was Warren Kump's annual Christmas gift to his wife.

In the beginning, Mother Teresa went out to plead for food, medicines, and funds in Calcutta. She enlisted Father Van Exem in gathering aid and in putting notices in local newspapers. A Calcutta resident related an incident of those early days when Mother Teresa went from office to office in search of funds. Most business people responded, but one man spat in her outstretched hand, saying "Take that!" "That was for me," she responded quietly, extending her other palm, "Now what about something for my children?"

I noted the change in her methods as I accompanied her to talks to groups in Calcutta, including high school students. These audiences belonged to various religious communities. After describing the needs of the children and the goodness of poor families, she would say, "This is a chance to do something beautiful for God," and leave it at that.

A Hindu businessman of great wealth, concerned about the fate of the sisters as they became ill or grew older, wanted to deposit an enormous sum in a bank on their behalf. He explained that the fund was not to be touched, but was to be allowed to draw interest until used at a later date. Mother Teresa told the businessman that while she was deeply grateful for this generous concern, she could not accept the donation. She could not keep money in the bank, she explained, while people died of starvation. The man was so moved that he made the gift without any conditions.

When the Missionaries of Charity arrived in New York, the Archdiocese offered to make a sum available to each sister every month toward her upkeep. The offer was turned down. Providence was all.

A second change concerned her outlook on poverty. Mother Teresa had dealt with the utmost in human want and physical suffering. After her experiences in the West, she stated, "The worst disease today is not leprosy; it is being unwanted, being left out, being forgotten. The greatest scourge is to forget the next person, to be so suffocated with things that we have no time for the lonely person, even a person in our own family who needs us.

"When our sisters were visiting the old people in Harlem, they came to a door and no one answered. The woman had been dead for days and no one knew—except for the odor in the hallway. So many are known only by the number on the door.

"Maybe if I had not picked up that one person dying on the street, I would not have picked up the thousands. We must think *'Ek'* [Bengali for *one*]. I think *'Ek, Ek.'* One, one. That is the way to begin."

THE PEACEMAKER

A third development in her views concerned war. When we first talked, I explained that many of us, influenced by Dorothy Day, had become "Sermon on the Mount" pacifists, refusing any part in war. But surely, she had replied, a country has the right to defend itself. She had known nothing but the tradition of the just war. As time went on, her defense of life so stunningly expressed in the Home for the Dying reached out to counter the growing tide of abortion. In her Nobel Prize acceptance speech she cited the first recognition of the Prince of Peace in the womb of Elizabeth.

"Let us not use bombs and guns to overcome the world," said Mother Teresa to nations pouring out the substance of their peoples on weapons of death. "Let us use love and compassion. Let us preach the peace of Christ as he did. He went about doing good....If everyone could see the image of God in his neighbor, do you think we should still need tanks and generals?"

When Dorothy Day and I visited Calcutta in 1970 as part of a round-the-world peace mission, Mother Teresa pinned the Missionary of Charity crucifix on Dorothy's left shoulder. "You are now a Missionary of Charity," she said. Dorothy had talked to the sisters gathered at the motherhouse about lay people in the Catholic Worker who choose not only poverty but gospel nonviolence, seeing Jesus in the enemy.

Mother Teresa's horror of war, and its reversal of the works of mercy and love, broke through her reserve over participating in political matters when the 1991 Gulf War became imminent. She addressed a long letter pleading "Please choose the way of peace," to President George Bush and Saddam Hussein. She wrote: "You have the power and the strength to destroy God's presence and image, his men, his women, and his children. Please listen to the will of God. God has created us to be loved by his love and not to be destroyed by our hatred. In the short term there may be winners and losers in this war that we all dread, but that never can and never will justify the suffering, pain, and loss of life which your weapons will cause. I come to you in the name of God, the God that we all love and share, to beg for the innocent ones, our poor of the world and those who will become poor because of war....You may win the war but what will the cost be on the people who are broken, disabled, and lost."

Shortly after the end of the Persian Gulf war, Mother Teresa was in the midst of the chaos in Iraq. Perhaps because of her letter, she was asked to bring in teams of sisters. The first team began work in a building behind the hospital of St. Raphael conducted by the Chaldean Catholics. "We are in the heart of Baghdad," she wrote. "The house is full of malnourished and crippled children. The need is so great. I do not know how long it will take to rebuild. I never thought that our presence would give so much joy to thousands of people—so much suffering everywhere."

GOING HOME TO GOD

In the fall of 1991 Mother Teresa, at age 81, started a journey from Calcutta that took her to Rome, Warsaw, New York, Washington, and San Francisco. In most of those cities she received young women who took vows as Missionaries of Charity, twenty-seven in Washington alone. Her next destination was Tijuana, Mexico, where there were Sisters and Missionary Fathers of Charity.

Then she collapsed. She had overtaxed a heart already functioning with aid of a pacemaker. Just as had been the case in 1983 in Rome and 1989 in Calcutta, there was once again worldwide anxiety about her survival. Press and television people converged on the Scripps Medical Center in La Jolla, to which she had been taken. Messages arrived from around the world, from heads of states, including President and Mrs. Bush. Radio and television bulletins featured interviews with her doctors. Would this be the time, to use Mother Teresa's words, when she would "go home to God"? Again questions were raised as to who would succeed her as mother general of the Missionaries of Charity. She had answered that years before. "Wait for Mother Teresa to die first. God will find someone as weak as I am to carry on his work." When she rallied, the doctors told her she would have to have more rest, to which she replied that she would have all eternity to rest.

In January 1992 she set out for Rome, accompanied by Joseph Langford, M.C., to present the constitution of the Missionary Fathers of Charity to the Holy Father. When we saw her on a short stopover in New York, she was frailer, more bent over than ever. Her eyes were alight, however, when she talked of the new houses in Albania and asked us for prayers for the entry of the sisters into China.

In Calcutta in September 1992, Mother Teresa had surgery to clear a blocked blood vessel and seemed close to death. Although she rallied once again and resumed her travels around the world to visit the houses of the Missionaries of Charity, she did not fully regain her strength. She was hospitalized several times in 1996 for renewed heart and breathing problems.

Last March her congregation acceded to her request, first voiced nearly ten years ago, to resign as its head; and they elected as her successor sixty-two-year-old Sister Nirmala Joshi, an Indian convert from Hinduism. In June Mother Teresa visited the Missionaries' convent in the South Bronx. While she was there she had a forty-five minute conversation with Princess Diana, who was also in New York City at that time.

Mother Teresa returned to Calcutta, where on the evening of September 5, she died of a massive heart attack, less than a week after the death of the Princess.

The Indian Government immediately announced that there would be a state funeral for Mother Teresa on September 13. When I heard that, I wondered, as I often had before, at the way this tiny, wrinkled, worn-out woman could evoke the world's concern.

What the world was responding to was a woman consumed by the gospel of Jesus, a woman living out all the beatitudes, but the very incarnation of one of them: "Blessed are the merciful." Mother Teresa took Jesus at his word and accepted him with unconditional love in those with whom he chose to be identified—the hungry, the shelterless, the suffering. She enveloped them in mercy. Mercy, after all, is only love under the aspect of need, love going out to meet the needs of the person loved.

Could not the life of our time be mightily changed for the better if millions of his followers took Jesus at his word?

EILEEN EGAN
AUGUST 20, 1998

Part II

Mother Teresa "On Prayer"

It was the apostles who asked Jesus: "Jesus, teach us how to pray"—because they saw Him so often pray and they knew that He was talking to His Father. What those hours of prayer must have been—we know only from that continual love of Jesus for His Father, "My Father!" And He taught His disciples a very simple way of talking to God Himself.

Before Jesus came, God was great in His majesty, great in His creation. And then when Jesus came He became one of us, because His Father loved the world so much that He gave His Son. And Jesus loved His Father, and He wanted us to learn to pray by loving one another as the Father has loved Him.

"I love you," He kept on saying, "as the Father loved you, love Him." And His love was the cross, His love was the bread of life. And He wants us to pray with a clean heart, with a simple heart, with a humble heart. "Unless

27

you become little children, you cannot learn to pray, you cannot enter heaven, you cannot see God." To become a little child means to be one with the Father, to love the Father, to be at peace with the Father, our Father.

Prayer is nothing but that being in the family, being one with the Father in the Son to the Holy Spirit. The love of the Father for His Son—the Holy Spirit. And the love, our love for the Father, through Jesus, His Son—filled with the Holy Spirit, is our union with God, and the fruit of that union with God, the fruit of that prayer—what we call prayer. We have given that name but actually prayer is nothing but that oneness with Christ.

As Saint Paul has said, "I live no longer I, but Christ lives in me." Christ prays in me, Christ works in me, Christ thinks in me, Christ looks through my eyes, Christ speaks through my words, Christ works with my hands, Christ walks with my feet, Christ loves with my heart. It is as Saint Paul's prayer stated, "I belong to Christ and nothing will separate me from the love of Christ." It was that oneness: oneness with God, oneness with the Master in the Holy Spirit.

And if we really want to pray we must first learn to listen, for in the silence of the heart God speaks. And to be able to hear that silence, to be able to hear God we need a clean heart; for a clean heart can see God, can hear God, can listen to God; and then only from the fullness of our heart can we speak to God. But we cannot speak unless we have listened, unless we have made that connection with God in the silence of our heart.

And so, prayer is not meant to be a torture, not meant to make us feel uneasy, is not meant to trouble us. It is something to look forward to, to talk to my Father, to talk to Jesus, the one to whom I belong: body, soul, mind, and heart.

And when times come when we can't pray, it is very simple: if Jesus is in my heart, let him pray, let me allow Him to pray in me, to talk to His Father in the silence of my heart. Since I cannot speak—He will speak; since I cannot pray—He will pray. That is why often we should say: "Jesus in my heart, I believe in your faithful love for me, I love you." And when we have nothing to give—let us give Him that nothingness. When we cannot pray—let us give that inability to Him. There is one more reason to let Him pray in us to the Father. Let us ask Him to pray in us, for no one knows the Father better than He. No one can pray better than Jesus. And if my heart is pure, if in my heart Jesus is alive, if my heart is a tabernacle of the living God to sanctify in grace: Jesus and I are one. He prays in me, He thinks in me, He works with me and through me, He uses my tongue to speak, He uses my brain to think, He uses my hands to touch Him in the broken body.

And for us who have the precious gift of Holy Communion every day, that contact with Christ is our prayer; that love for Christ, that joy in His presence, that surrender to His love for Christ, is our prayer. For prayer is nothing but that complete surrender, complete oneness with Christ.

And this is what makes us contemplatives in the heart of the world; for we are twenty-four hours then in His presence: in the hungry, in the naked, in the homeless, in the unwanted, unloved, uncared; for Jesus said: "Whatever you do to the least of my brethren, you do it to me."

Therefore doing it to Him, we are praying the work; for in doing it with Him, doing it for Him, doing it to Him, we are loving Him; and in loving Him we come more and more into that oneness with Him and we allow Him to live His life in us. And this living of Christ in us is holiness.

Excerpted from a talk given in Berlin, June 8, 1980

———

When Mother Teresa was asked if her people had been mountain people, she answered, "No, they were not. As far as we can know, they were city people. They say that we were peasants, but that is not true." Then she laughed, "But that does not matter. We are all peasants before God."

"How did they preserve their faith?" someone asked. She answered in two words, "By prayer."

———

Mother Teresa described the work of the Sisters of Calcutta in showing love to the abandoned and dying, to the lepers, to children deprived of schooling, to children discarded in dustbins. She told them that peace began right in their own homes. It was so easy, she said, to think of how one would work in Calcutta, and to miss the very person we are living with, a person near to us, who needs a loving word, who needs our loving help. It has to start right where people find themselves.

"Children," she said, "ask your parents to teach you how to pray. That is the beginning."

Part III

Prayers

1

SAINT FRANCIS OF ASSISI'S PRAYER FOR PEACE

Mother Teresa, as the years went by, more and more became a voice for peace and reverence for life, following in the footsteps of the great Saint Francis of Assisi. The habitual greeting of Brother Francis was "The Lord give you peace." His age was not the gentle age of innocence, but one in which violence was a dreadful reality, not only in wars between cities but in the Crusades. Francis not only released the members of his Third Order from the obligation to bear arms, but intervened for peace during the Crusades. During the bloodiest days of the Crusades, Francis with Brother Illuminato dared to enter the enemy lines to talk to the Sultan about Jesus. Here is Francis' prayer for peace:

Lord, make me a channel of your peace;
where there is hatred, let me sow love;
where there is injury, pardon;
where there is discord, let me sow harmony;
where there is error, let me bring truth;
where there is doubt, let me bring faith;
where there is despair, let me bring hope;
where there are shadows, let me bring light;
where there is sadness, let me bring joy.

Lord, grant that I may not so much seek to be consoled
as to console, to be understood as to understand, to be
loved as to love, for it is in giving that we receive, it is in
pardoning that we are pardoned, and it is dying that we
are born to eternal life. Amen.

2

Prayer for Friendship With God

Mother Teresa indicated that the loving presence of a forgiving God was available to everyone, free. "To speak immediately with the personal God" was what Mother Teresa was asking when she asked people to pray. She left behind the desire, not so much to touch her hand, as happens with other charismatic figures, but to speak immediately with the personal God who is so immediately present.

Let the sound of your voice echo always in my ears, good Jesus, so that I may learn how my heart, my mind, and my soul can love you. Let the innermost recesses of my heart embrace you, my one and only good, my sweet joy, my true friend.

3

PRAYER MANTRA FOR PEACE BY SATISH KUMAR

In London, Mother Teresa had been chosen from all the world's peacemakers to give the first recitation of a peace prayer. It was composed by Satish Kumar, a follower of Gandhi. He called it a peace mantra; a mantra, in the Hindu sense, is a repeated prayer that renews spiritual energy.

> *Lead me from death to life,*
> *from falsehood to truth;*
> *Lead me from despair to hope,*
> *from fear to trust;*
> *Lead me from hate to love,*
> *from war to peace;*
> *Let peace fill our hearts,*
> *our world, our universe.*
> *Amen.*

4

MOTHER TERESA'S JESUS MEDITATION

As Mother Teresa put it, it was only a minor accident on June 2, 1983, that brought her to the attention of doctors, who informed the world press that part of her treatment was for poor blood circulation and that the painkillers they had prescribed, she had refused to take. "She wants to offer up her sufferings to God," they stated. As her strength returned, Mother Teresa asked for pen and paper to write the fruit of her sickbed meditations. On June 19, she put on paper this litany:

Who Is Jesus to Me?
The Word made flesh.
The Bread of life.
The Victim offered on the cross.
The Sacrifice offered at the holy Mass for the sins
*   of the World and mine.*
The Way to be walked.
The Joy to be shared.
The Peace to be given.
The Leper—to wash his wounds.
The Beggar—to give him a smile.
The Drunkard—to listen to Him.
The Mental [Patient]—to protect Him.
The Little One—to embrace Him.
The Blind—to lead Him.
The Dumb—to speak for Him.

The Crippled—to walk with Him.

The Drug Addict—to befriend Him.

The Prostitute—to be removed from danger and befriended.

The Prisoner—to be visited.

The Old—to be served.

To me, Jesus is my God.

Jesus is my Spouse.

Jesus is my Life.

Jesus is my only Love.

Jesus is my all in all.

Jesus is my everything.

Jesus I love with my whole heart, with my whole being. I have given Him all, even my sins, and He has espoused me to Himself in tenderness and love. Now and for life I am the spouse of my crucified Spouse. Amen.

5

PEACE PRAYER AT NAGASAKI

On a visit to Japan, Mother Teresa visited Nagasaki, where the second nuclear bomb had been detonated on August 9, 1945. She wrote a peace prayer on the plane and on April 26, 1982, standing directly at the point where the bomb had exploded, prayed:

Eternal Father, in union with the suffering and passion of Christ which is being relived at every Mass—we offer you the pain and suffering caused by the atomic bomb in this place to thousands of people, and we implore you, Eternal Father, to protect the whole world from the pain and suffering nuclear war would bring to the people of Japan and to the whole world, already filled with so much fear and distrust and anxiety among nations. Eternal Father, have pity on us all. Amen.

6

PRAYER OF GREGORY OF NAZIANZEN

Mother Teresa gave voice to the ancient Christian tradition regarding poverty. A fourth-century saint, Gregory of Nazianzen, said: "Friends, let us not misuse God's gifts to us, or God will say: 'Be ashamed, you who keep to yourselves what belongs to others.' Imitate God's fairhandedness, and no one will be poor." Here is a prayer by that Apostle of the Poor:

Remember, O Lord, my poverty; forgive me my sins. The place where iniquity abounds, let your grace abound. Do not take away from your people the grace of the Holy Spirit. Have mercy on us, O God our Savior; have mercy on us, O God our Savior: give to your people singleness of heart. Amen.

7

PRAYER FOR RECONCILIATION

Among Mother Teresa's prescriptions for peace was the teaching of reconciliation before bringing a gift to the altar and the command against harboring anger. Mother Teresa was a voice for forgiveness and reconciliation, praying:

O Jesus, through your passion, teach us to forgive out of love, teach us to forget out of humility.
Help us to examine our hearts and see if there is any unforgiven hurt—or any unforgotten bitterness.
Allow the Holy Spirit to enter my spirit and remove all traces of anger.
Pour out your love, peace, and joy into our hearts in proportion to our emptying ourselves of self-indulgence, vanity, anger, and ambition.
Help us to willingly shoulder the cross of Christ. Amen.

8

Psalm for Deliverance

Behind the altar of the Motherhouse of the Sisters of Charity was a large crucifix with the words, *I Thirst*. These words recalled not only the words of Jesus on the cross, but his symbolic thirst for the love of humankind. The words also recall the sixty-ninth Psalm in the Hebrew Scriptures:

Save me, O God, for the waters have come up to my neck.
I am sunk in the miry depths where there is no foothold;
    I have come into deep waters, swept and engulfed
    by the flood.
I am weary from calling for help; my throat is hoarse and
    parched. My eyes have grown dim looking for my God.
More than the hairs of my head are those who hate me for
    no reason; mighty are those who attack me, many
    are my enemies without cause. What I did not steal
    I am forced to restore.
But I pray to you, O Lord, at a time most favorable to you.
    In your great love, O God, answer me with your
    unfailing help.
Rescue me, lest I sink in the mire; deliver me from the storm
    and the deep waters.
In your mercy, O Lord, give me a good answer; in your
    great compassion, turn to me.
Dishonor has driven me to despair; I looked for sympathy
    and there was none, for comforters and there was no one.
They gave me poison for food and vinegar to drink.

*May snares be set for them in their banquets and traps in
their sacred feasts.*

*But I myself am humbled and wounded; your salvation,
O God, will lift me up.*

*I will praise the name of God in song; I will glorify him
with thanksgiving....*

Let the lowly witness this and be glad.

You who seek God, may your hearts be revived.

*For the Lord hears the needy and does not despise those
in captivity.*

9

ACT OF CONTRITION

On retiring, sisters of the Missionaries of Charity recite an
act of contrition, asking pardon for the Creator for anything done during the day that might have been an offense.
Then it was time for sleep, generally by ten o'clock at night.

*O My God! I am heartily sorry for having offended Thee,
and I detest all my sins, because I dread the loss of heaven
and the pains of hell, but most of all because they offend
Thee, my God, who are all-good and deserving of all my
love. I firmly resolve, with the help of your grace, to confess my sins, to do penance, and to amend my life. Amen.*

10

PRAYER TO RADIATE CHRIST

It could not have been foreseen that from the Motherhouse in Calcutta, from there as heart and center, hundreds of chapels would be founded in an ever-widening circle. In less than two decades, the words *I Thirst* would appear in chapels planted in poor and sequestered corners of the world, from an aboriginal settlement in the outback of Australia to a gathering place for the sick and the helpless in Tanzania. One of the prayers recited before the chapel crucifix was "Radiating Christ," composed by John Henry Newman.

Dear Jesus,
Help me to spread your fragrance everywhere I am.
Fill my heart with your Spirit and your life.
Penetrate my being and take such hold
*   of me that my life becomes a*
*   radiation of your own life.*
Give your light through me and remain
*   in me in such a way that every soul*
*   I come in contact with can feel your presence in me.*
May people not see me, but see you in me.
Remain in me, so that I shine with your light,
*   and may others be illuminated by my light.*
All light will come from you, Oh Jesus.
*   Not even the smallest ray of light*
*   will be mine. You will illuminate*
*   others through me.*

Place on my lips your greatest praise,
illuminating others around me.
May I preach you with actions more
than with words, with the example
of my actions, with the visible light
of the love that comes from you
to my heart. Amen.

John Henry Newman

11

PRAYER FOR OBEDIENCE

While Mother Teresa was away, she asked that her Senior Sisters practice obedience: Prompt, simple, blind, cheerful, for Jesus was obedient unto death.

Dear Lord, Let me be one who takes blame, accusation,
or punishment from another as patiently as if it were
coming from myself.
Let me be one who obeys quietly when I am corrected,
confesses my fault humbly and makes amends
cheerfully.
Let me be one who is no hurry to make excuses,
but accepts the embarrassment and blame
for even those faults that I did not commit. Amen.

Saint Francis of Assisi

12

PRAYER UPON DRESSING

Each sister of Charity prays over her simple robes as she dresses each morning. Her plea is to spend the day in God's presence, living out her vow of service to the poor.

Dear Lord, as I put on this sari, I pray that this habit be a reminder of my separation from the world and its vanities.

Let the world be nothing to me and I nothing to the world.

Let it remind me of my baptismal robe and help me to keep my heart pure from sin just for today.

As I put on these sandals, I pledge of my own free will, dear Jesus, to follow You wherever You shall go in search of souls, at any cost to myself and out of pure love of You. Amen.

13

DEDICATION PRAYER TO THE SACRED HEART

Mother Teresa wrote to her sisters as she traveled to Rome to request pontifical recognition of her order. She gave instructions to begin a novena to the Sacred Heart, so that they would all be worthy of this great gift.

I offer myself to You, O Sacred Heart of my Jesus, with the intention that all my life, all my sufferings, all my actions, all my being are to be employed in loving You, adoring You, glorifying You. Would that my heart be consumed and reduced to ashes through the strength of its love for You! Why am I not all heart to love You, and all spirit to adore You? Grant, I beseech You, that henceforward I may love only You, and all things in You and for You.

Saint Margaret Mary Alacoque

14

PRAYER FOR CHARITY

Mother Teresa asked her Junior Sisters to practice charity: words, deeds, thoughts, desires, feelings—for Jesus always went about giving love to all.

O My God! I love you above all things, with my
    whole heart
and my whole soul, because You are all-good and
    worthy of all my love.
I forgive all who have injured me, and ask pardon of all
    whom I have injured. Amen.

15

Prayer Before Sleep

Before lying down to sleep, each sister of Charity who had prayed over her habit and sandals while dressing, for the day to be lived in the presence of God, examined her conscience, basing her questions on the four vows:

Dear Lord,
Do I realize that I am really rich when I
*   possess the Kingdom?*
Help me to reach that realization.
Am I really happy to be poor?
Help to make me so.
Do I make myself available precisely because
*   I am poor and am available for Christ?*
Help me to be so.
Is my obedience active and responsible and the
*   expression of my love for God?*
Help me to show it.
Do I pray at work?
Ensure that I do so.
Do I meet Christ in the distressing disguise
*   of the poor I serve?*
Help me to see your true face. Amen.

16

ANIMA CHRISTI

The Missionaries of Charity prayer book was a little manual printed on the cheapest of paper. It was printed in English as the common language of the Society. It contained such traditional prayers as the *Anima Christi*:

> *Soul of Christ, sanctify me,*
> *Body of Christ, save me,*
> *Blood of Christ, inebriate me,*
> *Water from the side of Christ, wash me,*
> *Passion of Christ, strengthen me,*
> *O Good Jesus, hear me,*
> *Within Thy wounds hide me,*
> *Suffer me not to be separated from Thee,*
> *From the malicious enemy defend me,*
> *In the hour of my death call me,*
> *And bid me come unto Thee,*
> *That with Thy Saints I may praise Thee,*
> *For ever and ever. Amen.*

17

PRAYER FOR POVERTY

Mother Teresa charged her novices to practice poverty: in desires, attachments, in likes and dislikes—for Jesus being rich made Himself poor for us.

Dear Lord, to follow in your footsteps, give us the grace to embrace your poverty above all other human commitments. Let us live our lives according to the poverty of our most high Lord, Jesus Christ and his most holy mother. Let us persevere in this to the last. Help us to keep close watch over ourselves, so that we never abandon this poverty through our own failings or through the advice or teachings of anyone.

Based on the Rule of Saint Francis

18

PRAYER FOR CHASTITY

From her Postulants, Mother Teresa requested sacrifices in the name of chastity: chastity in thoughts, affections, in desires and attachments, in avoiding idle conversations.

O Lord Jesus Christ, guardian of chaste souls, and lover of purity, who was pleased to take our nature and to be born of an Immaculate Virgin, mercifully look upon me and preserve my chastity. Create in me a clean heart, O God, and renew a right spirit within me. Help me to drive away impure thoughts, to conquer every sinful desire, so that, this temptation being overcome, I may serve You with a chaste body and a pure heart. Amen.

19

PRAYER OF GANDHI

In Calcutta is a figure of Gandhi standing on a fifteen-foot-high pedestal. He was carved holding the staff of a pilgrim. It had been in Bengal that he had walked from village to village as a pilgrim for peace between Muslim and Hindu. On the pedestal were Gandhi's prayerful words:

> *In the midst of death,*
> *life persists.*
> *In the midst of untruth,*
> *truth persists.*
> *In the midst of darkness,*
> *light persists.*
> *Hence, I gather that God is*
> *Life, Truth, and Light.*

20

PRAYER TO SECURE DIVINE PROVIDENCE

Often happy coincidences occurred with Mother Teresa when things just happened to be at the right place at the right time. Mother Teresa would attribute this to providence, in the sense that *Provisor providebit* (The Provider will provide). God, as the provider of all, has and will provide for his creatures, but there is a distinction between ordinary providence by which our daily needs are met, and extraordinary providence in which a totally unexpected or even wildly improbable answer materializes to meet a need. Mother Teresa seemed to make no distinction between ordinary and extraordinary providence. Almost every time she spoke, she called attention to the loving delicacy with which God reached down to meet human needs.

Providence of my God, I abandon myself to you without reserve. I place my destiny in your hands.

I confide to you the care of my body and my soul, my health and my reputation, my goods and my fortune, my life, my death, and especially my eternal salvation.

I no longer desire to govern myself but to be governed in all things by your providence. I will not give myself up to useless anxiety or unnecessary cares, but doing for my part what you command, I confide to you the success of all my undertakings.

*I will not undertake anything that I have not confided to
  your care, and in all difficulties and doubts I will have
  recourse to you as a never-failing source of help.*
*And so, peaceful and contented in all, I will live and die
  under the reign and the direction of your divine
  providence. Amen.*

Blessed John Martin Moye

21

PRAYER FOR THE COURAGE TO CARE

Mother Teresa served as the respondent on a panel on "Why
Should People Care?" One of the panelists was Elie Wiesel,
who as a child survived the extermination camp of
Auschwitz, scene of the murder of over four million human
beings. He pointed to indifference and forgetfulness of great
crimes like the Holocaust as a reason why more of mankind—even mankind itself—might fall victim to mass destruction. "The tale of what was done to my people," said
Wiesel, "can save mankind from a similar fate. Which means:
we must care—lest we fall victims to our own indifference."

*Give us courage, O Lord, to stand up and be counted, to
stand up for those who cannot stand up for themselves, to
stand up for ourselves when it is needful for us to do so.*

Let us fear nothing more than we fear Thee. Let us love nothing more than we love Thee, for thus we shall fear nothing also.

Let us have no other god before Thee, whether nation or state. Let us seek no other peace but the peace which is Thine.

Alan Paton

22

PRAYER IN HONOR OF THE HOLY CROSS

Mother Teresa told this story about visiting Yemen, a completely Muslim country. She told the prime minister of that country: "I am ready to give you the sisters under one condition, that you allow a priest to come also." Then the officials of Yemen consulted with each other and decided to allow the sisters to have priests. And then I was told, "Don't wear the cross." I went straight to the Governor and said to him, "What we are wearing, this is our sign. It is an external sign of our dedication. We belong to Him." They also did not want us to pray the rosary on the street. We pray the rosary on the street and it doesn't matter what street we are on. "This is our strength," I said, "We pray." Then he said, "You must remain. We have accepted you as you are, not as somebody else wants you to be." And today, the sisters are there with the cross and praying the rosary in the streets.

Lord Jesus Christ, for the sake of Your holy cross,
    be with me to shield me. Amen.
Lord Jesus Christ, by the memory of Your blessed cross,
    be within me to strengthen me. Amen.
Lord Jesus Christ, for Your holy cross, be ever round
    about me to protect me. Amen.
Lord Jesus Christ, for Your glorious cross, go before me
    to direct my steps. Amen.
Lord Jesus Christ, for Your adorable cross, come You
    after me to guard me. Amen.
Lord Jesus Christ, for Your cross, worthy of all praise,
    overshadow me to bless me. Amen.
Lord Jesus Christ, for Your noble cross, be You in me
    to lead me to Your kingdom. Amen.

23

Prayer to See Christ in Others

Mother Teresa once said that Jesus comes in so many forms, even so many disguises, that there was no difficulty in loving each person as a person. This echoes the words of the priest-poet, Gerard Manley Hopkins who, in his poetry, came close to catching the limitless fascination of Christ for those who lives were bound up with His:

Each mortal thing does one thing and the same:
Deals out that being indoors each one dwells;
Selves—goes itself; myself it speaks and spells,
Crying What I do is me: for that I came.

I say more: the just man justices;
Keeps grace: that keeps all his goings graces;
Acts in God's eye what in God's eye he is—
Christ—for Christ plays in ten thousand places,
Lovely in limbs, and lovely in eyes not his
To the Father through the features of men's faces.

Gerard Manley Hopkins

24

MARY'S *MAGNIFICAT*

In the Moghen David Synagogue of Calcutta, Mother Teresa said the prayer of Mary, a Jewish maiden:

My soul proclaims the greatness of the Lord,
my spirit exults in God my savior!
He has looked upon his servant in her lowliness,
and people forever will call me blessed.
The Mighty One has done great things for me,
Holy is his Name!
From age to age his mercy extends
to those who live in his presence.
He has acted with power and done wonders,
and scattered the proud with their plans.
He has put down the mighty from their thrones
and lifted up those who are downtrodden.
He has filled the hungry with good things
but he has sent the rich away empty.
He held out his hand to Israel, his servant
for he remembered his mercy,
even as he promised our fathers,
Abraham and his descendants forever.
Amen.

25

PRAYER TO LINK THE WORKS OF THE MISSIONARIES OF CHARITY TOGETHER

At the Third International Chapter of the Co-Workers of Mother Teresa in May 1982, sixty-five men and women came from thirty countries in Europe, Africa, Australia, and North and South America to meet as a family. As always, Mother Teresa was the heart of the meeting. She proposed that the Co-Workers in each country be called "links." She said, "I would rather like to use 'link'—like a branch, a joining." I would like the fifteenth chapter of Saint John (on the vine and the branches) to become our life." She wrote these prayerful words:

Dear Lord,
Let us become a true and faithful branch on the vine.
Let us accept You in our lives as it pleases You to come,
As the Truth—to be told;
As the Life—to be lived;
As the Light—to be lighted;
As the Love—to be loved;
As the Way—to be walked;
As the Joy—to be given;
As the Peace—to be spread;
As the Sacrifice—to be offered in our families
*   and with our close neighbors as well as those*
*   who are faraway.*

26

ALBERT'S SCHWEITZER'S PRAYER FOR PEACE

The Nobel Prize Committee awarded the Peace Prize for 1979, the Year of the Child, to Mother Teresa. The chairman of the Nobel Committee, Professor John Sannes said, "The Nobel Prize Committee considered it right and appropriate, precisely in this year, in their choice of Mother Teresa, to remind the world of the words spoken by Fridtjof Nansen: 'Love of one's neighbor is realistic policy.'" He continued, "As a description of Mother Teresa's lifework we might select the slogan that a previous Nobel Peace Prize Laureate, Albert Schweitzer, adopted as the leitmotif for his own work 'Reverence for Life.'" Here is a prayer by Albert Schweitzer from that book:

May this prayer unite us once more, so we know with each other and from each other the only one joy in life, the joy of which all other pleasures are but a reflection, the only joy capable of lightening our deepest misery: the peace of God which passeth all understanding, the union of our poor mortal wills with his will in deed and joy and sorrow, and that we shall pursue this peace together, for we shall then become ever richer and stronger in it, and able to show others the way.

Albert Schweitzer

27

PRAYER OF THANKSGIVING

The gold peace medal and diploma representing the prize and its gift of over $190,000 were placed in Mother Teresa's hands, and she was left alone in the spotlight. Her speech was undoubtedly the simplest Nobel response ever delivered in that academic hall. First, she led the entire assemblage in reciting the peace prayer attributed to Saint Francis of Assisi. Then she spoke to the audience, as usual without a note:

Let us all thank God for the joy of spreading peace, the joy of loving one another, and the joy of recognizing that the poorest of the poor are our brothers and sisters.

Let us thank God for the opportunity that we all have for this gift of peace that reminds us that we have been created to live that peace, that Jesus became man to bring that Good News to the poor. He being God became man in all things like us except sin, and He proclaimed very clearly that He had come to give the Good News. The news was peace to all men of good will, and this is something that we all want—the peace of heart. And God loved the world so much that He gave his son—it was a giving—it is as much as if to say it hurt God to give, because He loved the world so much that He gave his Son, and He gave Him to the Virgin Mary, and what did she do with Him?

As soon as Jesus came into her life, Mary went in haste

to give that Good News. As she came into the house of her cousin, the child—the unborn child—that child in the womb of Elizabeth, leapt with joy. It was that little unborn child who was the first messenger of peace. He recognized the Prince of Peace; he recognized that Christ had come to bring the Good News for you and me.

28

PRAYER FOR ENLIGHTENMENT

In August 1961, Mother Teresa announced a milestone for the Missionaries of Charity. She told the sisters that on October 7, 1961, they would have the first elections for the Chapter General. She suggested a special daily prayer for enlightenment.

Come, O Blessed Spirit of Knowledge and Light, and grant that I may perceive the Will of the Father; show me the nothingness of earthly things, that I may realize their vanity and use them only for Thy glory and my own salvation, looking ever beyond them to Thee and Thy eternal rewards.

29

PRAYER FOR THE SILVER JUBILEE OF THE MISSIONARIES OF CHARITY

In honor of the Twenty-fifth Jubilee of the Missionaries of Charity, a celebration was held at the Syrian Mar Thoma Church, the church which claims Saint Thomas the Apostle as its founder in southern India. This prayer greeted Mother Teresa:

O God of love and pity, we thank thee for all those who are engaged in the missionary task of thy Church. At this hour, we especially thank thee for thy guidance in the founding of the Society of the Missionaries of Charity. For the spiritual growth, for the strength to serve, for the increase of love and wisdom, and for all the blessings the sisters have received, through their service to the poor and the unwanted, we thank thee, O God.

30

BUDDHIST PRAYER FOR LIGHT

At the end of the Silver Jubilee Service at the Buddhist temple, the head monk of the Mahabodhi Society gave Mother Teresa two electric candles, one of which was placed with the sanctuary lamp in the convent chapel. Though Buddhists do not share the Christian belief in a personal God, they share the Christian commitment to mercy for one's fellow human beings. A Buddhist leader said that he saw Mother Teresa in the light of the *Bodhisattva*, the enlightened being, called "regarder of the cries of the world." She was also likened to a *Bodhisattva* because of her "joyful participation in the sorrows of humanity."

> *May I become a medicine for the sick and their physician,*
> *their support until sickness come not again.*
> *May I become an unfailing store for the wretched, and*
> *be first to supply them with their needs.*
> *My own self and my pleasures, my righteousness past,*
> *present, and future, may I sacrifice without regard, in*
> *order to achieve the welfare of all beings.*
> *With clasped hand I entreat the Enlightened Ones to kindle*
> *the lamp of mercy for them who in their blindness fall*
> *into sorrow.*

> *Santideva (c. A.D. 700)*

31

MEMORARES FOR MIRACLES

When the Congregation of the Missionaries of Charity had just been established, they urgently needed a building for the Congregation's Motherhouse. To get it, Mother Teresa promised the Virgin Mary to pray 85,000 *Memorares*. The Motherhouse was not long in coming.

Remember, O most gracious Virgin Mary,
that never was it known that anyone who
fled to your protection, implored your help,
or sought your intercession was left unaided.
Inspired by this confidence, I fly to you,
O virgin of virgins, my Mother. To you I
come, before you I stand, sinful and
sorrowful. O Mother of the Word Incarnate,
despise not my petitions, but in your mercy,
hear and answer me. Amen.

32

PRAYER TO OUR BLESSED VIRGIN

Mother Teresa recommends praying these words to Mary:

Mary, Mother of Jesus and of those who participate in his priestly ministry, we come to you with the same attitude of children who come to their mother.

We are no longer children, but adults who desire with all our hearts to be God's children.

Our human condition is weak, that is why we come to ask for your motherly aid so we are able to overcome our weakness.

Pray for us so that we can, in turn, become people of prayer.

We invoke your protection so that we may remain free from all sin.

We invoke your love so that it may reign and we will be able to be compassionate and forgiving.

We ask for your blessing so we can be like the image of your beloved Son, Our Lord and Savior, Jesus Christ. Amen.

33

PRAYER TO SAINT VINCENT DE PAUL

Mother Teresa once said: "I believe it was Saint Vincent de Paul who used to say to those who wanted to join his congregation: 'Never forget, my children, that the poor are our masters. That is why we should love them and serve them, with utter respect, and do what they bid us.'"

O glorious Saint Vincent, patron of all charitable associations and father of all who are in misery, while you were on earth you did never cast out any who came to you; come now to our assistance! Obtain from our Lord help for the poor, relief for the infirm, consolation for the afflicted, protection for the abandoned, a spirit of generosity for the rich, the grace of conversion for sinners, zeal for priests, peace for the Church, tranquility and order for all nations. Let all people benefit from the effects of your merciful intercession, so that, being helped by you in the miseries of this life, we may be united to you in the life to come, where there will be no more grief, nor weeping, nor sorrow, but joy and gladness and everlasting happiness. Amen.

34

PRAYER FOR FAITHFULNESS

It was a difficult beginning for Mother Teresa when she first left the Sisters of Loreto in Calcutta. Her first five homeless children had turned into twenty-five by the very next day. She experienced moments of terrible anguish and loneliness. Recalling those days, Mother Teresa said: "I had the feeling of how unbearable their poverty must be. While looking for a house or shelter, I would go searching without a destination, and my arms and legs would become exhausted. I thought how much the hearts and bodies of those who search for a house, food, or health must ache. The memory of the Convent of Loreto became a temptation for my spirit. I freed myself from that anguish by a heartfelt prayer."

My God, I choose freely
and because I love you,
I choose to remain faithful to my decision,
and to do only your will.

35

THE *OUR FATHER* OF SAINT FRANCIS OF ASSISI

The apostles did not know how to pray, and they asked Jesus to teach them. He, then, taught them the Our Father. Mother Teresa said, "I think that every time we say the Our Father, God looks at his hands, where we are etched. 'See, I have inscribed you on the palms of my hands…' (Isaiah 49:16). What a beautiful description and also expressive of the personal love God feels for each one of us." Here is Saint Francis of Assisi's version of the Our Father:

O most holy Pater Noster: our creator, redeemer, consoler, and savior.

Who art in heaven: in the angels and in the saints; enlightening them to know you, for you, O Lord, are light; enkindling them to love, for you, O Lord, are love dwelling in them and filling them with happiness, because you, Lord, are the highest Good, the eternal Good, from whom is every good; without whom there is no good.

Hallowed be thy name: may our knowledge of you ever increase in clarity, that we may know what is the breadth of your gifts, the length of your promises, the heights of your majesty, and the depth of your judgments.

Thy kingdom come: that you may reign in us through grace and make us come to your kingdom where there is clear vision of you, perfect love of you, blessed union with you, and everlasting enjoyment of you.

Thy will be done on earth as it is in heaven: to the end that we may love you with our whole heart by always thinking of you; with our whole soul by ever desiring you; with our whole mind by directing all our intentions to you, by seeking your honor in all things; and with all our strength by spending all our powers and senses of the body and soul in the service of your love and in nought else; and that we may love our neighbors even as ourselves, drawing all to your love to the best of our power; rejoicing in the good of others as in our own and giving compassion to them in their troubles while giving no offense to anyone.

Give us this day our daily bread: your beloved Son, our Lord Jesus Christ, that we may keep in mind and understand and revere the love which he had for us, and all that he taught us and did and suffered for us.

And forgive us our trespasses: out of your ineffable mercy, through the power of the passion of your beloved Son, and through the merits and intercession of the most Blessed Virgin and of all your elect.

As we forgive those who trespass against us: and what we do not fully forgive, do you, O Lord, make us forgive in full, that we may truly love our enemies for your sake and devotedly intercede for them before you, not rendering anyone evil for evil, but in you may we strive to be of help to all.

And lead us not into temptation: hidden or evident, sudden or persistent. But deliver us from evil, past, present, or to come. Amen.

36

PRAYER OF POPE PAUL VI

The bedrock of the association of the Co-Workers of Mother Teresa's Missionaries of Charity was prayer. They were asked to pray daily in unity with the sisters, a prayer which begged for the grace to merit serving the poor who were seen as the "ambassadors of God." Here is that prayer created by Pope Paul VI:

> *Make us worthy, Lord,*
> *To serve our fellowmen*
> *Throughout the world*
> *Who live and die in poverty*
> *   and hunger.*
> *Give them, through our hands,*
> *This day their daily bread;*
> *And by our understanding love,*
> *Give peace and joy.*
> *Amen.*

37

PRAYER FOR THE POOR

On her travels to France, in 1976, Mother Teresa stopped at the Burgundian village of Taizé where she was welcomed by the prior of the Ecumenical Center, Brother Roger Schutz. Brother Roger, a Protestant, had been given the blessing of Pope John XXIII to conduct a program looking toward the reconciliation of all Christians. Before leaving Taizé, Mother Teresa joined with Brother Roger in composing a prayer:

Oh God,
Father of each human being,
You ask each of us to carry love
To the places where the Church is brought low,
Reconciliation to the places where men are divided,
Father against son,
Mother against daughter,
Husband against wife,
The believer against those who find it impossible
    to believe,
The Christian against his unloved brother Christian.
You open the way for us,
So that the wounded Body of Jesus Christ, Your Church,
May become the leaven of Communion
For the Poor of the earth,
And the whole human family.
Amen.

38

PRAYER FOR JOY

One special mark of the Missionaries of Charity is their cheerfulness or joy. Part of the constitutions of the order are even devoted to this point.

> *Dear God,*
> *Let joy, which is the fruit of the Holy Spirit*
> *and a characteristic mark of the kingdom of God,*
> *Descend on us this day.*
> *For in Bethlehem the Angel said "Joy,"*
> *And Christ shared his joy with his apostles by saying,*
> *"That my joy may be with you,"*
> *For the word "joy" was the password*
> *of the early Christians,*
> *and Saint Paul often repeats,*
> *"Rejoice in the Lord always";*
> *For at Baptism the priest tells the newly baptized,*
> *"May you serve the Church joyfully."*
> *Let the joy as expressed in the Eucharist surround us*
> *and spread to all those whom we serve in love.*
> *Amen.*

39

PRAYER OF SAINT IGNATIUS LOYOLA

Following Indian custom, the Sisters of the Missionaries of Charity shed their sandals at the entrance of the chapel and padded their way barefoot into the chapel for a half-hour of prayer and meditation. After meditation the sisters recited from their prayer book a prayer of stark and total abandonment to the Lord by Saint Ignatius, founder of the Society of Jesus:

*Take, O Lord, and receive all our liberty, our memory,
    our understanding, and our whole will, whatever we
    have and possess.*

*You have given us all these; to you, O Lord, we restore
    them; all are yours, dispose of them in any way
    according to your Will. Give us your love and grace,
    for this is enough for us.*

Amen.

40

Litany of Loreto

Many prayers helped to form the days of the Missionaries of Charity. A regular feature consisted of reciting the traditional litanies of the Church. One special litany was that of Mary, the Mother of Jesus.

We fly to thy patronage, O holy Mother of God. Despise not our petitions in our necessities: but deliver us from all dangers, O ever glorious and blessed Virgin.

Lord, have mercy on us.
Christ, have mercy on us.
Lord, have mercy on us.
Christ, hear us.
Christ, graciously hear us.
God, the Father of heaven, have mercy on us.
God the Son, Redeemer of the world, have mercy on us.
God the Holy Spirit, have mercy on us.
Holy Trinity, one God, have mercy on us.

Holy Mary, pray for us.
Holy Mother of God, pray for us.
Holy Virgin of virgins, pray for us.
Mother of Christ, pray for us.
Mother of divine grace, pray for us.
Mother most pure, pray for us.
Mother most chaste, pray for us.

Mother inviolate, pray for us.
Mother undefiled, pray for us.
Mother most amiable, pray for us.
Mother most admirable, pray for us.
Mother of our Creator, pray for us.
Mother of our Savior, pray for us.
Virgin most prudent, pray for us.
Virgin most venerable, pray for us.
Virgin most renowned, pray for us.
Virgin most powerful, pray for us.
Virgin most merciful, pray for us.
Virgin most faithful, pray for us.
Mirror of justice, pray for us.
Seat of wisdom, pray for us.
Cause of our joy, pray for us.
Spiritual vessel, pray for us.
Vessel of honor, pray for us.
Singular vessel of devotion, pray for us.
Mystical rose, pray for us.
Tower of David, pray for us.
Tower of ivory, pray for us.
House of gold, pray for us.
Ark of the covenant, pray for us.
Gate of heaven, pray for us.
Morning star, pray for us.
Health of the sick, pray for us.
Refuge of sinners, pray for us.
Comforter of the afflicted, pray for us.
Help of Christians, pray for us.

Queen of Angels, pray for us.
Queen of Patriarchs, pray for us.
Queen of Prophets, pray for us.
Queen of Apostles, pray for us.
Queen of Martyrs, pray for us.
Queen of Confessors, pray for us.
Queen of Virgins, pray for us.
Queen of all Saints, pray for us.
Queen conceived without original sin, pray for us.
Queen of the most holy rosary, pray for us.

Lamb of God, who takes away the sins of the world,
    spare us, O Lord.
Lamb of God, who takes away the sins of the world,
    graciously hear us, O Lord.
Lamb of God, who takes away the sins of the world,
    have mercy on us.

Pray for us, O Holy Mother of God.
That we may be worthy of the promises of Christ.

Let us pray. Pour forth, we beseech you, O Lord, your
grace into our hearts, that as we have known the
Incarnation of Christ, Your Son by the message of an
Angel, so, by His Passion and Cross, we may be brought
to the glory of His Resurrection; through the same Christ
Our Lord. Amen.

May your divine assistance remain always with us. Amen.

41

PRAYER FOR VOCATIONS

The sisters around Mother Teresa, increasing in numbers each year from the Society's foundation in 1950, had become known as the "running sisters" as they moved swiftly to find and serve the poor, the rejected, the diseased, and the dying. In contrast, the decline in vocations to many other women's congregations became precipitous after the Second Vatican Council which ended in December 1965. Here is a prayer for vocations:

God, we thank you for the blessings you have given us in Christ, our Redeemer. Let your Spirit overshadow your people, making your gentle invitation heard in many hearts.

Lord of the harvest, bless your family throughout the world with many vocations, so that those in greatest need will experience the good news of redemption.

May your love grow among us and spread throughout all your creation,

Through Christ our Lord. Amen.

42

PRAYER OF RABINDRANATH TAGORE

Indian Prime Minister Indira Gandhi stressed Mother Teresa's identification with Indian culture when she presented her with an honorary doctorate from a university which arose from a school founded by Rabindranath Tagore, the Poet Laureate of India. Here is one of his poem-prayers:

This is my prayer to you, O Lord—strike at the root of
penury in my heart.
Give me the strength lightly to bear my joys
and sorrows.
Give me the strength to make my love fruitful in service.
Give me the strength never to disown the poor or bend
my knees before insolent might.
Give me the strength to raise my mind high above
daily trifles.
And give me the strength to surrender my strength to
your will with love.

Rabindranath Tagore

43

PRAYER FOR REMAINING "RIGHT ON THE GROUND"

The humility and concreteness of the Constitutions of the Missionaries of Charity came clearly from the heart and hands of a woman dealing humbly and concretely with the wounds and agonies of humankind. The pattern of working "right on the ground" manifested itself first in the city of Calcutta tormented by every form of suffering, every agony. It is brought to life in this prayer based on the prescriptions of Gandhi given in 1927:

Lord, let us start at the bottom, let us enter into what is best in the life of the poor and offer nothing that is inconsistent with it. Let that make our work more efficacious, and let what we say and offer to these people be appreciated without suspicion and hostility. Let us go to the poor, not as patrons, but as one of them, not to oblige them, but to serve them and work among them. Amen.

44

PRAYER OF SERVICE

Mother Teresa gave a talk to the Habitat Forum which took place in a rough hangar, part of a former army barracks. Extra benches of unpainted wood had been installed and on the highest ones, young people in jeans were singing. In the first rows were special guests, mostly in wheelchairs, some with necks held in metal braces. Sitting on the benches was a group of persons who were deaf and dumb. Mother Teresa began with a prayer, and as she spoke, a young girl translated the words into sign language.

Lord, make us worthy to serve the poor around the world who live and die in poverty and hunger. Let us serve the handicapped for we are all handicapped in one way or another. Sometimes it can be seen on the outside; sometimes on the inside. Let us come together not to plan any big thing, but to give to others until it hurts for the poor and needy enrich us and show us Jesus. Amen.

45

A PRAYER FOR THE FAMILY

Mother Teresa's way of life is one of dedication. But it is a life that anyone can live. Speaking to families, Mother Teresa emphases that love begins at home. Here are Mother Teresa's words in honor of families embodied in prayer:

Dear God of Joy,

Give me the grace to make my home another Nazareth where peace, love, and happiness reign. Let me love You through the love that is given to my family.

Let my mission of love begin in my own home, and then spread out to all who are in need of Your love and grace. Let Your love take root first in my heart and then in the hearts of all those with whom I come into contact.

Let my home be a center of kindness, compassion, and mercy. Give me the grace to make anyone who comes into contact with me go away better and happier.

Let the love I have given others, even in small ways, come back to me as Your grace. Let me forgive always and grant that this forgiveness will return to me and flourish.

Let me begin then in the place where I am, with the people I know, and let the lamp of Your love always shine in the windows of my heart and my home. Amen.

46

CONSECRATION PRAYER

In the profession ceremony, each sister-candidate came forward to present herself to Mother Teresa at the altar. She prays solemnly:

For the honor and glory of God and moved by a burning desire to quench the infinite thirst of Jesus on the cross for the love of souls,

by consecrating myself wholly to Him in total surrender, loving trust and cheerfulness,

here and now, I vow myself for life chastity, poverty, obedience, and wholehearted and free service to the poorest of the poor.

I give myself with my whole heart to this religious family, so that by the grace of the Holy Spirit and the help of the Immaculate Heart of Mary, the cause of our joy and Queen of the world,

I may be led to the perfect love of God and my neighbor and make the Church fully present to the world of today.

47

PRAYER FOR CONFORMANCE TO CHRIST

Mother Teresa settled down in the airport to read and ponder Alan Paton's *Instrument of Thy Peace*. This book of meditations inspired by the peace prayer of Saint Francis of Assisi was a favorite of hers and one she recommended to Co-Workers around the world.

O Lord, grant that we may not be conformed to the world, but may love it and serve it. Grant that we may never shrink from being the instruments of Thy peace because of the judgment of the world. Grant that we may love Thee without fear of the world, grant that we may never believe that the inexpressible majesty of Thyself may be found in any power of this earth. May we firstly love Thee and our neighbors as ourselves. May we remember the poor and the prisoner and the sick and the lonely, and the young searchers, and the tramps and vagabonds, and the lost and the lonely, as we remember Christ, who is in them all. And may we this coming day be able to do some work of peace for Thee. Amen.

Alan Paton

48

PRAYER TO SAINT DEMETRIUS

The marks of five centuries of Turkish rule and of Islamic presence were strong in the Skopje in which Mother Teresa spent her girlhood. The strength of the Albanian Christian identity can still be seen as it lives on in enclaves of Albanians who fled before the Turkish occupation. One such enclave occupies the Piana degli Albanesi near Palermo in Sicily. There the priests wear the stovepipe headpieces with flowing veil as worn by Orthodox priests, though these Albanians are in union with Rome, and their churches are bright with icons memorializing saints from their own history, including Saint Demetrius, the Great Martyr.

O Christ our God, you who gave the world Demetrius as a powerful protector against dangers and as an invincible soldier of Christ, arm us with his strength and make us perfect soldiers of Christ. Wherefore, O Great Martyr Demetrius, through your prayers, intercede with Christ our God that He may grant us his great mercy and save our souls. Amen.

Byzantine Daily Worship

49

PRAYER OF SAINT THÉRÈSE OF LISIEUX

On many occasions Mother Teresa was asked if her patron saint was Saint Teresa of Ávila, the Carmelite nun of sixteenth-century Spain, often called the "great" Saint Teresa. "Not the big Saint Teresa of Ávila," Mother Teresa always explained, "but the little one." Many echoes of Saint Thérèse are to be found in Mother Teresa's special vocation of love. Saint Thérèse's full religious name was Thérèse of the Child Jesus and the Holy Face of Christ. Here is one of her prayers:

O Jesus, who in your cruel passion did become the Man of Sorrows, I worship your Divine Face. Once it shone with the beauty and sweetness of the divinity; now for my sake it has become as the face of a leper.

Yet in that disfigured countenance, I recognize your infinite Love, and I am consumed with the desire to love you and make You loved by all humankind.

The tears that streamed in such abundance from your eyes are to me as precious as pearls, which I delight in gathering, that with their infinite worth they may be ransomed for the souls of poor sinners.

O Jesus, your face is the sole beauty that captures my heart. I cannot behold the sweetness of your glance here on earth, but I pray that you would imprint on me your Divine Likeness. I ask also that your Love may inflame and consume me, so that I soon may reach in heaven the vision of your Glorious Face. Amen.

50

Prayer to the Immaculate Heart of Mary

Mother Teresa called the pilgrim's shelter Nirmal Hriday, Bengali for Pure or Immaculate Heart. It was named in honor of the Virgin Mary since it was opened in 1952 on the feast day dedicated to Mary's Immaculate Heart.

O Pure and immaculate blessed Virgin, who are the sinless Mother of your Lord, you who are the hope of the hopeless and sinful, we sing your praises. We bless you, as full of every grace, you who did bear the God-Man; we invoke you and implore your aid. Rescue us, O holy and inviolate Virgin, from every necessity that presses in on us and from all temptations. Be our intercessor and advocate at the hour of death; deliver us from the outer darkness; make us worthy of the glory of your Son, O dearest and most clement Virgin Mother. You indeed are our only hope most sure in God's sight, to whom be honor and glory for ever and ever, world without end. Amen.

Saint Ephrem the Syrian

51

ROSARY PRAYER

The date of the acceptance of the Missionaries of Charity as a new congregation limited to the diocese of Calcutta was October 7, 1950, a feast dedicated to Our Lady of the Rosary. By 1958, the Missionaries of Charity, few as they were, had become an accepted feature on the streets of Calcutta, reciting the rosary and praying their way, even on trams. "Now they tell me," said Mother Teresa, "the time that it takes to reach different places by the number of rosaries they can say. When they pray as they go along, the people see it and respect them. In India there is a great respect for holiness, even among the rascals."

Queen of the Most Holy Rosary, in these secular times of indifference, show your power with the signs of your ancient victories, and from your throne, from which you dispense pardon and graces, mercifully regard the Church of your Son. Hasten the hour of mercy, and for me, who am the least among human beings, kneeling before you in prayer, obtain the grace I need to live righteously upon the earth. In company of all the faithful Christians throughout the world, I salute you and acclaim you as Queen of the Most Holy Rosary. Amen.

52

Litany of Humility

The Sisters of the Missionaries of Charity said a special litany for every day of the week. Monday's litany was that of the Holy Spirit. Tuesday's litany was of particular interest, since it was the litany of humility, attributed to Cardinal Merry del Val of Spain.

Change my heart, O Lord, You who have been brought to nothing for love of me! Reveal to my spirit the excellence of Your holy humiliations. Enlightened by Your light, may I begin today to destroy any pride that is wholly alive in me! This is the source of my miseries, the standing obstacle which I oppose to Your love! Lord, I am my own enemy when I seek peace in myself and outside of You.

O Jesus, meek and humble of heart, hear me.

From the desire of being esteemed, Jesus deliver me.

From the desire of being loved, Jesus deliver me.

From the desire of being sought after, Jesus deliver me.

From the desire of being honored, Jesus deliver me.

From the desire of being praised, Jesus deliver me.

From the desire of being preferred to others, Jesus deliver me.

From the desire of being consulted, Jesus deliver me.

From the desire of being approved, Jesus deliver me.

From the fear of being humbled, Jesus deliver me.

From the fear of being despised, Jesus deliver me.

From the fear of suffering rebuffs, Jesus deliver me.

From the fear of being calumniated, Jesus deliver me.

From the fear of being forgotten, Jesus deliver me.

From the fear of being ridiculed, Jesus deliver me.

From the fear of being injured, Jesus deliver me.

From the fear of being suspected, Jesus deliver me.

Jesus, grant me the grace to wish:

That others may be loved more than I,

*That others may increase in the opinion of the world
and I diminish,*

That others may be employed and I set aside,

That others may be praised and I overlooked,

That others may be preferred before me in everything,

*That others may be more holy than I, provided I am as
holy as I can be.*

Cardinal Merry del Val

53

PRAYER FOR RECONCILIATION

On one of the first truck convoys to enter Bangladesh at the end of its two-week war for independence from Pakistan was Mother Teresa. "We saw the most terrible sufferings in Bangladesh. Our sisters started right away to help. But the greatest need in Bangladesh," she said slowly, "is for forgiveness. You have no idea how these people have suffered. There is so much bitterness and hatred left. Perhaps if they believed that people cared about them, if they felt loved, they could find it in their hearts to forgive what was done to them. I think this is the only thing that can bring peace."

To you, Creator of nature and humanity, I pray:

Hear my voice, for it is the voice of the victims of all wars and violence among individuals and nations.

Hear my voice, for it is the voice of all children who suffer and will suffer when people put their faith in weapons and war.

Hear my voice, for I speak for the multitudes in every country and in every period of history who do not want war and are ready to walk the road of peace.

Hear my voice and grant insight and strength so that we may always respond to hatred with love, to injustice with total dedication to justice, to need with the sharing of self, to war with peace.

O God, hear my voice, and grant unto the world your everlasting peace. Amen.

Pope John Paul II

54

PRAYER FOR UNDERSTANDING THE HOLY EUCHARIST

As Mother Teresa was to say repeatedly, the lives of the sisters were "woven about the Eucharist," the commemoration of the Last Supper when Jesus offered Himself as the victim for the sin of the world. The central act of the liturgy of the Catholic Church, so often attended listlessly as a Sunday duty by church members, becomes in the Motherhouse on Lower Circular Road, the fulcrum about which the whole day turns.

What blessing, or what praise, or what thanksgiving, can we render to You, O God, the Lover of all persons, for that when we were cast away by the doom of death, and drowned in the depth of sin, You did grant us freedom, and bestowed on us the immortal, the Heavenly Food, and manifested to us this Mystery, hid from ages and from generations? This Eucharist, Your supreme act of mercy, and the greatness of your generosity and Fatherly care for us, grant us to understand. Amen.

Saint Cyril of Alexandria

55

PRAYER FOR MARTYRDOM

At a stopover in Munich, Mother Teresa accepted a suggestion to take a few hours and visit nearby Dachau, the forerunner of all the concentration camps that pockmarked occupied Europe. Soon Mother Teresa was standing before a gas chamber disguised as a shower room. As she moved to walk between rows of blockhouses left standing as a reminder of what had occurred on the blood-soaked acres of hundreds of concentrations camps. She was told that at least 2,579 priest-inmates had perished at Dachau alone. Among the priests who perished in concentration camps was a Carmelite, Père Jacques Bunol, who said this following prayer by Saint Thérèse of Lisieux every morning while imprisoned in Mauthausen:

O my God! O blessed Trinity! I desire to love you and to make You loved. I desire to fulfill Your will perfectly. In a word, I desire to be a saint, but I feel my powerlessness, and I ask You Yourself to be my sanctity.

In my heart I feel immense desires and it is with confidence that I ask You to come and take possession of my soul. Dwell in me, as in the tabernacle; do not ever leave me.

I console You for the ingratitude of the wicked. I beg You to take away the liberty to displease You.

I thank You, O my God, for all the graces You have granted me, especially for having tried me in the crucible of suffering. I do not wish to store up merits for heaven, I want to work for Your love alone, with the single goal of pleasing You, of bringing consolation to Your Sacred Heart and of saving souls whom You will love eternally.

In the twilight of this life, I shall appear before You with empty hands, for I do not ask You, Lord, to compare my works. All our justices are tainted in Your eyes. Hence I wish to wear the cloak of Your Justice, and receive from Your love eternal possession of You. I wish no other crown or throne but You, my Beloved.

So that my life may be an act of perfect love, I offer myself as the victim of holocaust to Your merciful love, begging You continuously to consume me, allowing the floods of infinite tenderness which are obtained in You to overflow in my soul so that I thus become a martyr to Your love.

May this martyrdom, after having prepared me to appear before You, at last let me die and may my soul, without delay, soar to the eternal embrace of Your merciful love.

I wish, O my Beloved, with each beat of my heart to renew this offering an infinite number of times until the shadows have vanished.

Saint Thérèse of Lisieux

56

PRAYER OF LOVE

Human beings wanted to know if they mattered in the scheme of things. They seemed to want to hear it from someone who needed nothing from them, nothing at all. They heard it from a poor and powerless woman who had plumbed the very depths of human agony and who traveled about the world with a tiny cloth bag containing her two saris, writing letters on the rough, lined copybook of the poorest school child. They listened when they heard that despite massive evidence of human cruelty, there was a force of love that was stronger, and that they could be a part of it. Mother Teresa's presence made them aware of the stream of love that the Creator poured over all his creation and of their place in it. Thomas Merton, the Cistercian monk, put it in a few words: "To say that I am made in the image of God is to say that love is the reason for my existence, for God is love."

You have taught us that if we are open to one another,
*   you dwell in us.*
Help us to preserve this openness.
Help us to realize that there can be no understanding
*   where there is mutual rejection.*
O God, in accepting one another wholeheartedly, fully,
*   completely,*
we accept you, and we thank you;
and we love you with our whole being,

because our being is in your being,
our spirit is rooted in your Spirit.
Fill us then with love,
and let us be bound together with love as we go
our diverse ways,
united in this one Spirit which makes you present
to the world.

Thomas Merton

57

PRAYER OF GOOD INTENTION

A woman was wheeled in for a talk with Mother Teresa. She was a victim of cerebral palsy; her body by pragmatic standards was "useless." She said, "We can never obtain complete happiness on earth for happiness is found only in heaven. And we cannot obtain it if we give in to our despair. We are fortunate to have a share in Christ's cross." She suggested this prayer:

Give us this day the grace to live now as you intend, dear
God; to smile even when our burdens seem heavy and our
hearts seem broken. Let us be charitable and humble in
humiliation and in our inconveniences. Above all, O Mer-
ciful Lord, let us suffer without regret, for in your will, and
in our gracious acceptance of that same holy will, lives
our eternal destiny. Thanks be to God. Amen.

58

LEGION OF MARY PRAYER

Michael Gomes, a gentle Bengali teacher, provided the first home for the Missionaries of Charity at 14 Creek Lane in Calcutta. The young order was housed in a large upper room that ranged the length of the three-story house. Michael Gomes took no money from Mother Teresa. He himself was a devout member of an association called the Legion of Mary, founded in Dublin by Frank Duff. Its purpose is to express by whatever means possible Christian concern for one's neighbors and is grounded in a regular program of prayer. Here is a prayer from the Legion of Mary Handbook:

Confer, O Lord, on us,
Who serve beneath the standard of Mary,
That fullness of faith in You and trust in her,
To which it is given to conquer the world.
Grant us a lively faith, animated by charity,
Which will enable us to perform all our actions
From the motive of pure love of You,
And ever to see You and serve You in our neighbor;
A faith, firm and immovable as a rock,
Through which we shall rest tranquil and steadfast
Amid the crosses, toils, and disappointments of life;
A courageous faith which will inspire us
To undertake and carry out without hesitation
Great things for God and for the salvation of souls;
A faith to lead us forth united—

To kindle everywhere the fires of Divine Love—
To enlighten those who are in darkness and in the
shadow of death—
To inflame those who are lukewarm—
To bring back life to those who are dead in sin;
And which will guide our own feet in the Way of Peace.

Legion of Mary Handbook

59

PRAYER TO SAINT FRANCIS XAVIER

In 1964 Mother Teresa opened a house in Goa on the west coast of India, and a relic of Portugal's colonialization. There the Missionaries of Charity were given the care of the chapel of Saint Francis Xavier, Jesuit missionary to India.

O Great Saint Francis, well-beloved and full of charity, with you I reverently adore the Divine Majesty. I especially rejoice in the singular gifts of grace bestowed on you during your life. I give thanks to God, and beg of you, with all the affections of my heart, that by your powerful intercession you may obtain for me the grace to live a holy life and die a holy death. Moreover, I beg of you to obtain for me any special spiritual or earthly favors for which I pray, but if what I ask does not tend to the glory of God, and the greater good of my soul, I beseech you, obtain for me what will more certainly reach these ends. Amen.

60

PRAYER FROM SAINT IGNATIUS LOYOLA'S
SPIRITUAL EXERCISES

The parish of the Sacred Heart in Skopje was a pivotal influence in the life of the young woman who was later known as Mother Teresa. A Jesuit priest introduced the young people of Sacred Heart to the Sodality of the Blessed Virgin Mary. This organization was founded in 1563 among the lay students in the Roman college of the Society of Jesus (Jesuits). Agnes Gonxha Bojaxhiu and her friends were given the words of Saint Ignatius as a challenge: "What have I done for Christ? What am I doing for Christ? What will I do for Christ?" Here is a prayer from Ignatius' *Spiritual Exercises* that echoes this challenge:

Here I am, O King and Lord of all things: I, so unworthy, but still confiding in your grace and help, I offer myself entirely to You and submit all that is mine to Your will. In the presence of Your infinite Goodness, and under the sight of Your glorious Virgin Mother and of the whole heavenly court, I declare that this is my intention, my desire, and my firm decision: Provided it will be for Your greatest praise and for my best obedience to You, to follow You as nearly as possible and to imitate You in bearing injustices and adversities, with true poverty, of spirit and things as well. Amen.

61

PRAYER FOR THE PROPAGATION OF THE FAITH

While in New York City, Mother Teresa visited the office of Bishop Fulton J. Sheen, at that time nationally known for his television programs on ethics in daily living. He was head of the American section of the foreign mission organization called the Propagation of the Faith. A man of powerful presence and singular dramatic gifts, he summoned his entire staff to pray together with a woman who stood for the poor of the earth.

Eternal Father, by your infinite mercy and by the infinite merits of your divine Son Jesus, make yourself known and loved by all souls, since it is your will that all should be saved.

Through the sacred mysteries of human redemption send, O Lord, laborers into your harvest.

Eternal Word incarnate, Redeemer of the human race, convert all souls to yourself, since for them You were obedient even unto your death on the cross.

Through the merits and intercession of your most holy Mother and of all the angels and saints, send, O Lord, laborers into your vineyard. Amen.

62

Prayer of Australia's First Peoples

Through the quiet influence of James Robert Knox, who served as Melbourne's archbishop from 1967 until called to Rome in 1974, the Missionaries of Charity arrived in 1969 to start work in Australia. After visiting the native peoples of Australia, the aborigines, Mother Teresa accepted the call to serve the needs of Australia's first peoples.

O God, you are my God;
Always will I seek you.
My soul thirsts for you,
My flesh longs for you.
As the eagle belongs in the air,
As the dolphin belongs to the sea,
As the wolf belongs to the land,
So we belong to you, O God, my God.

O God, God of all peoples everywhere,
Please enable us to forgive each other.
Make us people who will walk and live together
In genuine acceptance and respect for each other.
In Jesus' name and for his sake. Amen.

63

PRAYER OF ONE HEART

In the continents of Europe, Australia, and Africa, and the troubled ridge between East and West, the Missionaries of Charity were putting flesh on a vision, a vision caught from the charism of Mother Teresa. It was articulated in a communication on rough mimeographed paper that was regularly circulated among the sisters all around the world. It was a sharing of their experiences among the world's poorest and was called *Ek Dil*, an expression describing the unity among the sisters in their far-flung houses. *Ek Dil* in Hindi stands for "One Heart."

O most loving Jesus, we pray You, by the sweetness of Your Divine Heart, convert the sinner, console the suffering, help the dying, and lighten the pains of the souls in purgatory. Make all our hearts one in the bonds of true peace and love, and grant us a holy and peaceful death. Amen.

64

PRAYER OF THE LITTLE SISTERS OF THE POOR

Mother Teresa saw the urgent need for the institutions that had grown out of the Christian presence in India, in particular, the educational institutions for women, the hospitals, and leprosariums. Lay Christian women and sisters formed the heart of the Indian nursing corps. Mother Teresa herself had first been part of the work of education and then had profited from the hospitality and training at the Holy Family Hospital in Patna. She revered the work of the Little Sisters of the Poor who in the beginning had given her shelter among the aged poor in their care.

Mary, we have chosen you for our Mother. Never have you had such unworthy children as we are, nor ones so weak and frail. Therefore, be our strength and support. We have no resources and often no funds. O compassionate Mother! Grant that we may always find bread for your beloved poor. We are like defenseless children, exposed to the evils of the world. Grant that we may not be destroyed, but that we may live for the glory of God, and that we may spread His Word according to His will. Amen.

Jeanne Jugan, Founder of the Little Sisters of the Poor

65

PRAYER OF SUFFERING IN THE CROWN OF THORNS

Mother Teresa carried one souvenir from Las Vegas when she visited that city in 1960 to speak to a meeting of the National Council of Catholic Women. To give her time to meditate before her talk, she was driven into the Nevada desert. She settled by herself near a cactus plant for contemplation. At last, she picked up a few of the long cactus spines which were easily twined into a crown of thorns. This she took back to Calcutta where it was placed on the head of the crucified Christ hanging behind the altar in the novitiate chapel.

Wondrously fruitful thing, white, red, and black, is the noble crown of thorns pressed down upon the head of Christ. The white and spotless flesh of Christ defies the crime of Adam, red is the flower of the passion, and black is the death brought by His suffering.

O garland of thorns, comfort us in the blood of Christ; bind us, O belt of thorns, in a belt of virtue, that the sly serpent strike us not without showing himself.

And thou, O Jesus, do make of your crown our diadem, that we may be washed pure of all of our sins. Amen.

Ambrosian Liturgy

66

PRAYER OF SOR JUANA INEZ DE LA CRUZ

In 1975, Mother Teresa found herself in Mexico City as a member of the Vatican delegation to the World Conference of the International Women's Year. The program cover for the conference featured a picture of a seventeenth-century nun, Sor Juana Inez de la Cruz, a Sister of the Convent of Saint Jerome in Mexico City. Recognized by many as a true genius, Sister Juana Inez de la Cruz had studied, on her own, theology, the Bible, history, mathematics, and law. When she put forward a criticism of a priestly sermon, she was severely reprimanded by the bishop, who asserted that she should engage in "more suitable pursuits than those of the mind." Her reply was a twenty-thousand-word defense of woman as a person and of her right to education. In obedience to the bishop, however, Sister Juana Inez de la Cruz gave up her library. She died soon afterward while caring for people during a plague.

My God,

Instead of studying books, let me instead study all the things that you have created, taking them for my letters, and taking for my books all the intricate structures of the world.

Let me see nothing without reflecting upon You, let me hear nothing without pondering You, even the most minute and material things.

For there is no creature, however lowly, in which one
    cannot recognize the great "God made me"; there is
    not one that does not stagger the mind.
Let me look and marvel at all things that show bright
    traces and representations of You. Amen.

                    Adapted from The Answer/La Respuesta
                    by Sor Juana Inez de la Cruz

67

PRAYER FOR THE MIRACLE OF GOD'S LOVE

Mother Teresa was asked if she had ever seen a miracle. She replied, "There is a sort of miracle every day. There is not a day without some sign of His love, like the time we ran out of food because of floods. Just then the schools closed in Calcutta and all the bread was given to us so that the people would not go hungry. For two days, our poor had bread until they could eat no more. The greatest miracle is that God can work through nothings, small things like us. He uses us to do His work."

Our Father, here I am, at your disposal, your child,
use me to continue your loving the world,
by giving Jesus to me and through me,
to each other and to the world.
Let us pray for each other that we allow Jesus to love in us
and through us with the love with which His Father
loves him. Amen.

68

PRAYER OF FATHER MIGUEL PRO, S.J., IN HONOR OF THE FEAST OF CHRIST THE KING

In Mexico, Mother Teresa visited the cemetery where the martyr Miguel Pro was buried. For Mother Teresa, it was a chance to kneel in silent prayer for the Jesuit priest who had been executed during the anti-Catholic persecutions of Mexico.

Return to the Sanctuary, O Lord,
To the empty Tabernacle that awaits you.
Hear, O good Jesus, the cry
Of loving souls during their Calvary!
Attend the cry of crucified souls
On their cross of pain and sorrow.
For what greater grief can come our way
Than the lack of your divine presence?
Sweet Savior, why did you depart?
From the depths of our sorrow and desolation
We cry to you, O Lord, will you not hear us?
O God, you forgive those who confess their faults
And humbly acclaim you King!

Those who wounded you by their sins,
Now turn to you, repentant, Lord.
See them humbly implore your pardon.
By the tears of those who suffer for you,
Sweet Savior, return to thy Sanctuary!

69

PRAYER OF THE JAINS

October 1975 marked the Silver Jubilee of the Missionaries of Charity. To celebrate, every major religious group in Calcutta held their own commemorative service. The Jains carry the teaching of noninjury to its furthest extreme, applying nonviolence to insect, bird, man, and beast. For them, liberation from the cycle of rebirth comes from asceticism and solicitude for all living beings. At the temple of the Jains, the congregation recited a prayer of one of the founders of Jainism.

May I never cause pain to any living being,
May I never utter untruth,
And may I never covet the wealth or wife of another.
May I never drink the nectar of contentment...
May there be mutual love in the world,
May delusion dwell at a distance...
May all understand the Laws of Truth and joyfully
sorrow and suffering endure.
Peace.
Shanti,
Peace.

70

Prayer of the Stations of the Cross

In answer to a last-minute call, Mother Teresa was asked to give a talk to a group of young people who had for a year concentrated on performing works of mercy for the sick, the needy, and the lonely. Mother Teresa began her talk with the sign of the cross and the words, "Jesus said to the people of his time, 'If you want to be My disciples, take up your cross and come follow me.'" She went on to talk of the passion of Christ and of the stations of the cross by which Jesus made his way to the place of crucifixion.

Jesus lives His passion today in the suffering, in the hungry, in the handicapped—in that child who eats a piece of bread crumb by crumb, because when that piece of bread is finished, there will be no more, and hunger will come again. That is a station of the cross. Let us be there, Lord, with that child.

Jesus lives His passion today in the thousands who die not only for a piece of bread, but for a little bit of love, of recognition. That is a station of the cross. Let us be there, Lord, with those who are dying for love.

Jesus lives His passion today in the fall of the young people who, as Jesus did, fall again and again. Let us be there, Lord, like Simon Cyrene, to pick them up, to be at that station of the cross.

Jesus lives His passion today in the homeless people in the parks, the alcoholics and the drug-addicted. Let us not be one of those who look and do not see. Instead, Lord, let us be there at that station of the cross.

Jesus lives His passion when our people are disowned, thrown out, and racked with suffering. Let us, Lord, remain with these, our people, like Mary who stayed with Him when he was spat upon, treated like a leper, disowned by all, and crucified. Give us the eyes of compassion and the steadfastness of Mary who stayed with Jesus even when his followers deserted Him. Let us be there, Lord, at every station of the cross.

Give us the strength, Lord, to begin the stations of the cross step by sep. Satisfy our own hunger by the living bread of life, by your Holy Eucharist. Give us strength to give. Amen.

71

The Prayer of "Come and See"

As explained in the constitutions of the Missionaries of Charity Brothers, "a period of introduction to the life and novitiate will be called the time of 'Come and See,' on the pattern of Jesus calling His first followers." The young men were soon called the "Come-and-Sees," to distinguish them from the brothers who had taken vows.

O Lord, You who said, "What are you looking for?" grant me the grace to perceive and know what I ought to do for your sake.

O Lord, You who said, "Come and see," I come to you now to find the peace of my true home, grant me safety within the walls of your love.

O Lord, You who said, "Come to me—I am the vine and you are the branches," I come to you now as a fruitful branch on the tree of life.

O Lord, You who said, "Follow me," I come to You now as a faithful pilgrim on the path that you have set out for me.

O Lord, You who said, "Taste and see," I come to You to quench my thirst and eat the food of life eternal. Amen.

72

PRAYER OF DOM HELDER CAMARA

Mother Teresa was a magnetic figure at the forty-first Eucharistic Congress which addressed the spiritual and physical hunger of humankind. At the opening session, Mother Teresa seemed to stand for all the hungry of the world and the need to break bread with them. Over a table of round loaves, she recited a prayer, then broke the bread and shared it. Among those taking part were Dom Helder Camara, archbishop of Olinda-Recife, Brazil. The Congress was the occasion for the first appearance together of Dom Helder Camara and Mother Teresa, both identified as voices of the world's poor and rejected.

> *Holy breathing of God,*
> *I feel You stirring.*
> *Warmed by this breath, good things start to grow.*
> *Even in strong, wealthy lands,*
> *fresh, mobilizing calls evoke planetary piety,*
> *winning the hearts and the hands of the caring:*
> *each in her chosen path,*
> *each with his special gift,*
> *take their stand*
> *to create a world more fit for living,*
> *more just and more humane.*
>
> *Dom Helder Camara*

73

Prayer of Compassion

The covenants for the International Association of the Co-Workers of Mother Teresa were drawn up on March 23, 1969, in Rome. The Co-Workers consisted of men, women, young people, and children of all religions and denominations throughout the world, "who seek to love God in their fellowmen, through wholehearted service to the poorest of the poor," and who "wish to unite themselves in a spirit of prayer and sacrifice with the work of Mother Teresa and the Missionaries of Charity."

There were to be no dues. Meetings were to be held without the serving of food so that they could be held in the homes of the poor. Only water could be served. Sharing and prayer were to mark the gatherings of the Co-Workers. "Sharing" referred to experiences of compassion and a deeper reflection on them so that, in Mother Teresa's words, "Co-Workers could be enriched by each other."

By 1993 there were branches of the Co-Workers in seventy-nine countries. In that year, Mother Teresa wrote to the national "links" asking the Co-Workers to simplify their activities even further—no governing body, no bank accounts, no international meetings. Sick and Suffering Co-Workers everywhere will support the work by uniting their suffering with the work of the sisters and with the people they serve.

Sister M. Nirmala writes to the Co-Workers as did Mother Teresa, confirming them in their spiritual motivation. She wrote in April 1998, seven months after Mother Teresa had "gone home to God," "Dearest Co-Workers, you are a very important part of our Missionaries of Charity family and you have the same call as the M.C. Sisters, Brothers, and Fathers to become saints, great saints and to help others also to be so by your loving and courageous fidelity to His will for you in your own walk of life."

Make me, O Lord, the instrument of Thy love, that I may bring comfort to those who sorrow and joy to those who are regarded as persons of little account. In this country of many races make me courteous to those who are humble and understanding to those who are resentful. Teach me what I should be to the arrogant, the cruel, for I do not know.

And as for me myself, make me more joyful than I am, especially if this is needed for the sake of others. Let me remember by many experiences of joy and thankfulness, especially those that endure. And may I this coming day do some work of peace for thee.

Alan Paton

74

Prayer of Oscar Romero

One of the works of the Brothers of the Missionaries of Charity stationed in El Salvador was visiting the sick in poor families and giving or finding medical aid. They also learned how to build *champas* for people made homeless by the continuing violence in the countryside.

One day one of these brothers disappeared. It was soon discovered that he had been kidnapped and was being held as a hostage. The brothers went to Archbishop Oscar Romero to ask for help. Through the archbishop's intervention the brother was released. Three months later in March 1980, Archbishop Romero, the archbishop of San Salvador, was assassinated with a bullet to the heart as he was celebrating Mass.

It is not my poor word that sows hope and faith.
I am no more than God's humble echo in his people,
　　speaking to those chosen as God's scourges,
　　　who practice violence in so many ways.
　But let them beware.
　　When God no longer needs them,
　He will cast them into the fire.
　Let them instead be converted in time.
　And to those who suffer the scourges
　　and do not understand the why
of the injustices and abuses:

Have faith. Give yourselves,
will and mind and heart, entire.
God has his time.

Oscar Romero

75

PRAYER FOR SAFE TRAVEL

On one occasion, Mother Teresa was being driven at breakneck speed through the heart of Chicago to catch a plane. Her countenance never changed; she sat calmly with her rosary beads in her hand. She never started a journey without a prayer, asking the protection of God and the intercession of Mary.

We entreat you, Oh Lord, to turn your face toward us and protect us on our journey. Guide us in bringing your Good News to all whom we meet; and let us greet the poor and the afflicted with kindness and compassion. Mary, Our Mother, keep us safe and send us joy as we travel in the paths of the Lord. Amen.

76

PRAYER OF THE SUFFERING

Jacqueline de Decker embodied a special strand of Mother Teresa's life and was the "link" with those described in the constitution of the Co-Workers as "the sick and those unable to join in activities may become a close Co-Worker of an individual sister or brother by offering their prayers and sufferings for each sister and brother."

Jacqueline de Decker was the first to become spiritually bound with the Society and to find other handicapped people who would offer up their sufferings for a Missionary of Charity. So began a program which united two great mysteries, the mystery of the redemptive power of innocent suffering and the mystery of what has been called the "communion of saints." This communion is seen as transcending all physical barriers in the spiritual union of all human being of good will, human beings desiring to unite their wills with that of the Creator.

God, we yearn for your compassionate voice.
Your mercy testifies to your love.
Listen to our plea.
God, you always sustain the needy,
*   and hear the plea of the forsaken;*
*   let there be comfort for those who suffer.*
Give strength and faith to those who call unto you,
*   endurance and patience to those who need it.*

May your presence shine upon them always.
Without your help there is no comfort or cure,
  nor the means to relieve the weak and the suffering.
Hear this petition, O God of Compassion, and have mercy;
  alleviate the pain of those who suffer,
  so that they may rise and bless
  your infinite kindness. Amen.

Hugo Schlesinger and Humberto Porto

77

PRAYER OF PERSEVERANCE

The sisters at the Home for the Dying in Varanasi were serving not simply the destitute of the area but the poorest of the pilgrims in what was to them the holiest of cities. The sisters fed helpless old men, gently turning heads so that they could more easily swallow the food, and then cleaning away the food that escaped. They had to do this every day, bolstered by a short prayer of Mother Teresa's.

    Lord, give me this vision of faith,
    So that my work will not become monotonous.

78

Prayer for Kindness

In a letter to the Co-Workers, Mother Teresa advised them to be kind to each other in your homes. Be kind to those who surround you. I prefer that you make mistakes in kindness rather than you work miracles with unkindness. Often one word, one look, one quick action, can fill the heart of the one we love" with darkness.

Keep me, O God, from pettiness.
Let us be large in thought, word, and deed.
Let us be done with fault-finding and leave off self-seeking.
May we put away all pretense and meet each other face to
*   face without self-pity and without prejudice.*

May we never be hasty in judgment and always generous.
*   Let us take time for all things.*
*   Make us grow calm, serene, gentle.*

Teach us to put into action our better impulses and make us
straightforward and unafraid.

Grant that we may realize that it is the little things in life
that create differences; that in the big things we are all one.

And, O Lord God, let us not forget to be kind. Amen.

Mary Stuart, Queen of Scots

79

PRAYER FOR THE HUNGRY

A plain hall of the ancient Camaldolese Benedictine Monastery of San Gregorio on the Coelian Hill of Rome was the scene of the Third International Chapter of the Co-Workers of Mother Teresa in May, 1982.

The monastery and church of San Gregorio honored Pope Saint Gregory who from this spot dispatched a band of monks to evangelize England. They had set out nearly fourteen hundred years earlier, carrying with them precious gospel texts, holy books, and sacred vessels. In the Chapel of San Andrea was the very marble table, the "table of the poor," from which Saint Gregory and his mother, Saint Sylvia, had personally fed the hungry of sacked and gutted Rome. In the monastery itself, Mother Teresa's sisters conducted a shelter for the aged and the homeless. Their convent consisted of outbuildings that had been converted from chicken coops.

To allow the hungry to remain hungry would be blasphemy against God and one's neighbor, for what is nearest to God is precisely the need of one's neighbor. It is for the love of Christ, which belongs as much to the hungry as to myself, that I share my bread with them and that I share my dwelling with the homeless. Let me provide the hungry with bread. Let me prepare the way for your grace. Amen.

Dietrich Bonhoeffer

80

Prayer to Overcome Fear

Mother Teresa reminded the Co-Workers of the two words that heralded the coming of Jesus: "Fear not." She said, "There will be suffering, and more and more people are suffering in every country. There is that terrible fear of war....But such a fear is not for you. We will pray. We will pray. Prayer cannot fail, and not only pray, but put that prayer into a loving action, and do something for somebody."

My Lord Jesus, do not be far from me,
but come quickly and help me
for I am terrified by fears of the future.
How shall I break their power over me?
How shall I go unhurt without your help?
O Lord,
you have promised,
"I myself will prepare your way,
leveling mountains and hills.
I will open the gates of the prison,
and reveal to you
the hidden treasures of spiritual knowledge."
O Lord, do as you have said,
drive away all my fears.
This is my hope and my only comfort—
to turn to you,
to put all my trust in you,

to call inwardly upon you,

and to wait for your comfort with patience.

Thomas à Kempis, The Imitation of Christ, adapted

81

PRAYER TO PRESERVE THE LIFE OF THE UNBORN

Mother Teresa said "Today the greatest destroyer of peace is abortion. We who are standing here—our parents wanted us. Our children, we want them, we love them, but what of the millions? Many people are very concerned about the children of India, the children of Africa, where quite a number die, maybe of malnutrition, of hunger, and so on, but millions are dying deliberately by the will of the mother. And that is the greatest destroyer of peace today."

God, who in Isaiah, says very clearly that "even if a mother could forget her child—I will not forget you—I have carved you in the palm of my hand, carve all unborn children in the palm of Your hand. Keep them so close to you that their lives are never threatened by abortion. Give them lives of love and joy and keep them safe until they have given their service in this world. Protect all life in the womb with your strength and protection. Amen.

82

MARTIN LUTHER'S PRAYER FOR LASTING PEACE

The cavernous Lutheran Domkirche of Oslo was filled for the service of intercession on the occasion of Mother Teresa's visit to receive the Nobel Prize. Besides scriptural readings and hymns, there was a long litany of prayers for the poor, the suffering, and the victims of disaster in the whole world. The printed program was in Norwegian and English, but the congregation intoned, "Lord hear our prayer" in many tongues. The Lutheran bishop had invited John William Gran, the Catholic bishop of Oslo to preside with him at the altar, and joining with them were representatives of the Greek Orthodox Church, the Anglican Church, and Baptists, Methodists, and the Salvation Army.

Dear God, give us peaceful hearts and a right courage in confusion and strife. And so may we not only endure and finally triumph, but also have peace in the midst of the struggle. May we praise and thank you and not complain or become impatient against your divine will. Let peace win the victory in our hearts, that we may never through impatience initiate anything against you, our God, or our neighbors. May we remain quiet and peaceable toward God and toward other people, both inwardly and outwardly, until the final and eternal peace shall come. Amen.

Martin Luther

83

PRAYER TO SAINT LUCIA

As the celebrants left the service at the Lutheran Cathedral on that icy winter night, lighted torches were put into their hands and a procession formed to the Norwegian Mission Society where the Lutheran women's association had laid out a supper in the mission hall. As Mother Teresa entered the hall, a chorus of a hundred young girls, holding candles like a band of Christmas angels, welcomed her with a hymn and prayer to Saint Lucia.

O Lucy, martyr and bride of Christ, take us under your powerful protection. Your name signifies Light; guide us through the dark night of this life. O fair Lucy, light of virgins, pray for us that our blindness be healed, and that we may be able to see that true Light in the Child who was born at Bethlehem. By your intercession, O Lucy, secure our firmness of faith and enlightenment of soul. Amen.

84

PRAYER TO AVERT SUICIDES

In Rome, on December 14, Mother Teresa made her first visit to the Roman catacombs. After her tour of the tombs and the celebration of Mass, Mother Teresa said a few words. She began: "Here we are in a place where people loved God so much that they were ready to die for that love; men, women, and even little children. We have just seen the grave of a martyred child. They had hope in the Resurrection."

Then she said gravely, "What went through my mind was the temptation to suicide by so many people today. Let us pray for them that they will realize that they are loved by God. Let us pray that they may learn to love and to overcome the temptation to take their lives."

O God,
You who know the moment of our death,
You who know the moment of our creation,
We pray to You.
Bless this person contemplating suicide
and preserve this life of your child.
Turn the depths of this person's depression away
from self-destruction
and infuse him with your Holy Breath of Your Life.
Uncover for him the joys of the life you have set
out for him,
and grant him hope and confidence in Your love
and mercy. Amen.

85

PRAYER TO THE HEART OF JESUS

In answer to the probing question of a journalist, Mother Teresa made one of her rare and most succinct statements about her own identity. The journalist had pointed out that she was born in Yugoslavia and lived in India, while her sisters worked all over the world. Then the journalist asked, "And you, Mother Teresa, how do you feel about yourself?"

"By blood and origin," she replied, "I am all Albanian. My citizenship is Indian. I am a Catholic nun. As to my calling, I belong to the whole world. As to my heart, I belong entirely to the heart of Jesus."

> *Hail, Heart of my Jesus, save me.*
> *Hail, Heart of my Creator, perfect me.*
> *Hail, Heart of my Savior, deliver me.*
> *Hail, Heart of my Judge, pardon me.*
> *Hail, Heart of my Father, govern me.*
> *Hail, Heart of my Master, teach me.*
> *Hail, Heart of my King, crown me.*
> *Hail, Heart of my Benefactor, enrich me.*
> *Hail, Heart of my Brother, stay with me.*
> *Hail, Heart of my Incomparable Goodness,*
>   *have mercy on me.*
> *Hail, most Loving Heart, inflame me. Amen.*
>
> Saint Margaret Mary Alacoque

86

Prayer of Abandonment to God

Mother Teresa insisted on the need to become holy. She wrote, "The first step to becoming holy is to will it. As Saint Thomas says, 'Sanctity consists in nothing else than a firm resolve—the heroic act of a soul abandoning itself to God.' By an upright will we love God, we choose God, we run toward God, we reach Him, we possess Him."

Father, I abandon myself into your hands.
Abandonment is committed only with and in the
    maturity of Christ Jesus.
It is a letting go.
It is a severing of the strings by which one manipulates,
    controls,
    administrates,
    the forces in one's life.
Abandonment is managing nothing,
    expecting nothing.
Abandonment is receiving all things the way
    one receives
        a gift
    with opened hands,
    an opened heart.
Abandonment is being driven, directed, not
    by human needs,
        but by God's needs.

Abandonment is more than commitment.
It is deeper.
It is not doing anything for God
   but being done by God.
It is not only accepting a final crucifixion,
   allowing one's flesh to be eaten,
     one's blood to be spilt,
but to have the very cause,
   the reason,
   the mission,
   the work,
   the people
for which one's life was offered
   be made anathema, annihilated,
   if such be God's desire.
Abandonment holds God to no promises.
Abandonment is done not for the reward of one's
   resurrection,
     but only in hope that God's life
       encompass all things,
       that His Kingdom come,
       that His Will be done.

                      Edward J. Farrell, Disciples and Other Strangers

87

PRAYER OF BLESSING FOR WATER

Mother Teresa did not require any special foods. She seemed to appreciate cool, clean water most of all and when given a glass would bless herself before drinking it. One could not help thinking of Francis' canticle, "Praised be you, my Lord, for Sister Water, which is very useful and humble and precious and chaste."

Lord, O Lord, good Father, guardian of all earthly
*   things, look upon us with favor.*
Grant us the gift of Jordan's waters and shower us
*   with the blessings of the Holy Spirit.*
So be it.
Give us a saintly water.
So be it.
Give us a water that cleanses sin.
So be it.
Give us a water that regenerates and protects.
So be it.
Give us a living water that quenches our thirst and
*   our hearts. So be it.*

Ethiopic Liturgy, adapted

88

PRAYER OF JULIAN OF NORWICH

Mother Teresa's lightness of spirit reminded people of Julian of Norwich, who stated that the worst had already happened and had already been remedied—meaning the original sin and the remedy of Jesus in becoming man and dying for sin. Though there was the cross, there was always solace and joy in the resurrection that was its inevitable sequel. Mother Teresa seemed to be saying with Julian, "All shall be well, and all, all shall be well."

My Lord who said,
"All shall be well,"
and
"All manner of things shall be well,"
Give me faith in your word that all things will be saved.
Grant me the grace to understand that not even the smallest
*   things will be forgotten.*
Grant me the grace to take heed now,
*   faithfully and trustfully,*
and at the last end
see that all will be well
in your truth and the fullness of your joy.
Amen.

Julian of Norwich, adapted

89

PRAYER FOR SMILES

Mother Teresa often gave people unexpected advice. When a group of Americans visited her in Calcutta, they asked her for some advice to take home to their families.

"Smile at your wives," she told them. "Smile at your husbands."

Thinking perhaps that the advice was simplistic, coming from an unmarried person, one of them asked, "Are you married?"

"Yes," she replied to their surprise, "and I find it very hard sometimes to smile at Jesus. He can be very demanding."

Lord, renew my spirit and draw my face into smiles of delight at the richness of Your blessings. Daily let my eyes smile at the care and companionship of my family and community. Daily let my heart smile at the joys and sorrows that we share. Daily let my mouth smile with the laughter and rejoicing in Your works. Daily let my face give testimony to the gladness You give me. Thank you for this gift. Amen.

90

PRAYER FOR EMPTINESS OF SELF

Of all Mother Teresa's qualities, the one most overpower-ingly impressive to those close to her was, paradoxically, her emptiness. Mother Teresa asked her sisters to be "clear as glass," and she led the way. It was as though she had no needs of her own, but rather was an empty reed through which the Spirit blew.

Lord,
My soul is so dry that by itself it cannot pray;
Yet You can squeeze from it the juice of a thousand
*   prayers.*
My soul is so parched that by itself it cannot love;
Yet You can draw from it boundless love for you and for
*   my neighbor.*
My soul is so cold that by itself it has no joy;
Yet You can light the fire of heavenly joy within me.
My soul is so feeble that by itself it has no faith;
Yet by your power my faith grows to a great height.
Thank You for prayer, for love, for joy, for faith;
Let me always be prayerful, loving, joyful, faithful.

Guigo the Carthusian

91

CORPUS CHRISTI PRAYER

Mother Teresa's closeness to the Eucharist was no less than that of Francis of Assisi, who wrote, "If the tomb wherein Jesus reposed for a few hours is the object of such veneration, then how worthy, virtuous and holy ought he to be who touches with his fingers, receives in his mouth and in his heart, Christ, no longer mortal, but eternally triumphant and glorious." Mother Teresa's promotion of the Corpus Christi movement was an expression of this devotion to the Eucharist.

Behold, most loving Jesus, to what an excess your boundless love has carried You. Of your own flesh and precious blood you have made ready for me a divine banquet in order to give yourself to me. What impelled you to this act of love? It was your heart, your loving heart. Within the burning furnace of your Divine Love, receive my soul, that I may learn to be worthy of the love of that God who has given me such wondrous proofs of his love. Amen.

92

BLESSING FOR PEACE

Mother Teresa's appearance in Belfast at Corrymeela occurred in 1981. Corrymeela means "Hill of Harmony" in Gaelic, and was founded as a community of reconciliation for the bereaved on both sides of the conflict in Northern Ireland.

The blessings of God be to thee,
The blessings of Christ be to thee,
The blessings of the Holy Spirit be to thee,
And to thy children,
And to thee and to thy children's children.

The peace of God be to thee,
The peace of Christ be to thee,
The peace of the Holy Spirit be to thee,
During all the hours of thy day,
During all the days of thy life.

Gaelic Blessing

Sources and Acknowledgments

The excerpts in this book are adapted from *Such a Vision of the Street: Mother Teresa—The Spirit and the Work* by Eileen Egan and originally published by Doubleday in 1985. Other prayers have been taken or adapted from the sources that follow.

Anders, Isabel, ed., *Simple Blessings for Sacred Moments,* Liguori, Mo.: Liguori Publications. Used by permission.

Buehrle, Marie C., *Rafael, Cardinal Merry del Val*, Houston: Lumen Christi Press, 1980.

Camara, Dom Helder, *It's Midnight, Lord*, Washington, D.C.: The Pastoral Press, 1984.

Carden, John, compiler, *A World at Prayer*, Mystic, Connecticut: Twenty-Third Publications, 1990.

Chakravarty, Amiya, editor, *A Tagore Reader*, Boston: Beacon Press, 1961.

Chiffolo, Anthony F., *At Prayer With the Saints*, Liguori, Mo.: Liguori Publications, 1998. Used With Permission.

Christian Community Bible, Liguori, Mo.: Liguori Publications, 1995.

The Complete Book of Christian Prayer, New York: Continuum Publishing Company, 1996.

de la Cruz, Sor Juana Inés, *The Answer/La Respuesta*, translated by Electa Arenal and Amanda Powell, New York: The Feminist Press, 1994.

de Nola, Alfonso, compiler, *The Prayers of Man*, translated by Rex Benedict, London: Heinemann, 1962.

Dragon, A., S.J., *Blessed Miguel Pro: Martyr of Christ the King,* Mexico City: Buena Prensa, 1959.

Farrell, Edward, *Disciples and Other Strangers,* Denville, N.J.: Dimension Books, 1974. Used by permission.

González-Balado, José Luis, *Mother Teresa: Always the Poor,* Liguori, Mo.: Liguori Publications, 1980. Used by permission.

Guéranger, Prosper, The Liturgical Year: Advent, translated by Laurence Shepherd, St. Louis: B. Herder, 1895.

Ignatius Loyola, *The Spiritual Exercises,* translated by Pierre Wolf, Liguori, Mo.: Liguori/Triumph, 1997. Used by permission.

Julian of Norwich, *The Revelation of Divine Love,* translated by M. L. del Mastro, Liguori, Mo.: Liguori/Triumph. Used by permission.

Leroy, A., *History of The Little Sisters of the Poor,* London: R. & T. Washbourne, 1906.

The Official Handbook of the Legion of Mary, Dublin: Concilium Legionis Mariae, 1953.

Raya, Joseph and José de Vink, *Byzantine Daily Worship,* Allendale, N.J.: Alleluia Press, 1969.

Romero, Oscar, *Oscar Romero: The Violence of Love,* translated by James R. Brockman, S.J., Farmington, Pa.: Plough Publishing, 1998.

Paton, Alan, *Instrument of Thy Peace.* New York: The Seabury Press, 1968. "Give Us Courage, O Lord," "Make Me, O Lord, Thy Instrument," and "O Lord, Grant That We May Not Be Conformed to the World." Used by permission.

St. John, Ambrose, *The Raccolta.* London: Burns, Oates & Washbourne, 1924.

Schlesinger, Hugo and Humberto Porto, *Prayers of Blessing and Praise for All Occasions,* Mystic, Connecticut: Twenty-Third Publications, 1987.

Schweitzer, Albert, *Reverence for Life,* translated by Reginald H. Fuller, New York: Harper & Row, 1969.

Index of Prayers